THE (Z) FACTOR

SALES ACCELERATOR

ZFactor Group

Austin, TX

Request for permission to duplicate items should be emailed to:

ZFactor Group (A LeaderXY Company): permission@leaderxy.com

ISBN-13: 978-1477698754
ISNB-10: 1477698752

To order bulk quantities of this book,:

- Email: bulkorders@zfactorgroup.com
- Online: www.zfactorgroup.com
- Phone: 512-258-8352

ZFactor Group: Printed in United States of America
www.zfactorgroup.com

Cover Design and Graphics: Eric King, King+Sons Design
www.kingandsons.com

Let us hear from you about your experience with ZFactor.

Please go to our website:

www.zfactorgroup.com

Here more about ZFactor on the radio show: *Two Old Sales Guys and the Sales Diva Blogtalk Radio Show*

www.blogtalkradio.com/two-old-sales-guys-and-diva

Voiceover: David Dauber
daviddauber.voice123.com

Products and Services

- ZFactor Books

- ZFactor Online Platform for Sales Acceleration

- ZFactor Coaching

- ZFactor Coach Certification

- Sales Consulting & Advisory

Upcoming Books

- ZFactor: Sales Managers

- ZFactor: Crowdfunding

- ZFactor: Financial Professionals

- ZFactor: Faith-Work Integration

- Niche market books customized to specific industries. Contact us if interested in collaborating.

CONTENTS

ACKNOWLEDGEMENTS

I have written thousands of pages over the years—but never have put them into a book of this sort complete with inspiration, collaboration and content from the genius and lives of those around me.

The Thinking Framework™ Methodology, presented in this book, is the inspiration and work of my husband, Alan. This *'framework thinking'* has been integrated into our lives in one form or the other over the last twelve years. Our conversations are a constant interplay of life, business and how to serve those around us—and so there is no separation of this way of thinking from who we have become. It is my great hope, that we will touch many lives through ZFactor. I am grateful for his inspiration, collaboration and support to make this book a reality.

Bethany UMC is where the framework first became integrated into training courses. A team of us created the *Servant Leader Framework* for helping grow leaders in our church community (X axis = Spiritual Development and Y = Leadership Development). I want to acknowledge the contributions of Pastor Tom Deviney, Pastor David Minnich, Pastor Ed Wilder, John Robertson, and Dick Baumgartner for their partnership in the development of the framework methodology…I learned a lot and the foundation of that process has served me well.

ZFactor came alive for me and for the application specifically to sales in the last eight years. The 'play grounds' for testing and delivering the methodology were at both HotLink and Boundless (both Jason Black companies). Any theory has to be implemented in a live setting to be validated, and Jason and Henrik Johansson (co-founder Boundless) have supported many tools and resources to that end for our sales professionals—ZFactor being one of those. I appreciate this commitment and how their support of ZFactor, and me, has helped us create and continue to refine a strategic focus on creating value for clients and our company.

In particular, I want to thank and acknowledged Anna Miller, who worked with me at Boundless starting in 2006 to roll out a formal training complete with tracking and reporting that validated the framework process for sales. It was during this time the framework we were using was first called ZFactor to describe the journey we thought folks should take through the quadrants for product sales. Hundreds of hours have gone into ZMaps, coaching, trainings, client calls and webinars to explore the power of helping folks think and thus act differently—and ultimately sell differently to produce better results. I also want to thank Tom Rizzi, Jason Walker, and Nancy Grimes, who have been instrumental in supporting the use of ZFactor culturally within our sales organization.

I want to thank my cheerleaders…the folks whose unending encouragement, love and support and willingness to try a new way of thinking has done more to encourage me to *just do this* than I can ever express. I can't name everyone of course, but if I missed someone—I am hopeful that those who have contributed to my life will know my love and respect for them. So thank you—Amber George, Annette Hawkins, Carol Stone, Cheryl Scott-Pugh, Cheryl Cohen, The women of EWF, Haven Bey, Linda Caponigro, Liz Cavitt, Maria Hale, Mark Sweet, Melissa Anthony-Sinn, Michael Dominguez, Mom and Dad Gautschy, Noel Garcia, Ronne Rock, Theresa Roberts, Tyler Harrison, Terri and David Dauber and Valerie Savage—for your deep contributions to me personally and professionally.

Thank you to Tom and Kathi Ackerman who collaborated with us on the first ZFactor book targeted for Insurance Professionals. They have contributed untold hours and mindshare toward the ZFactor Sales Accelerator concept and the possibilities of the methodology overall.

And in closing:

May these words of my mouth and this meditation of my heart be pleasing in your sight, LORD, my Rock and my Redeemer. Psalm 19:14

Cindy G. Goldsberry
August 5, 2012

Foreword

by Jason Black

May 19, 1968 at 7:23 AM in Austin, Texas… Jason Andrew Black was born and "my seed" was planted.

I have a passionate belief that everyone has an opportunity to achieve greatness. I am a sap for reality TV shows like The Biggest Loser, where people completely transform their lives by pushing themselves and following a formula. Quite inspiring!

When we are born (the seed is planted), we are all on an equal playing field. Some seeds will turn out to mere onion plants while others will become mighty olive trees. What we choose to do and the decisions we make going forward determine our growth and our future. So my question for you…

There is no easy path to success. The journey to success is fraught with people with big ideas and dreams. What separates the winners from the losers is often the combination of "working hard and working smart." Working hard, well that should be the easy part of the formula. Unfortunately, however, many people are soft and full of excuses of "why it is too hard." The more difficult part of the equation is an acquired and disciplined learning called working smart.

Mastering the "work smart" formula requires the combination of art and science on top of a foundation of hard work. The work smart formula enables you to maximize your time, maximize your skill and maximize your earnings. Over the last 8 years at Boundless, we have been executing the ZFactor within our team and the results speak to the success:

- Fastest growing distributor amongst 18,000 players.
- $60,000,000 in revenue in 6 years.
- Highest percentage of year over year growth amongst the largest 40 distributors.
- 100's of happy sales professionals that are maximizing their income.

"Mastering the 'work smart' formula requires the combination of art and science on top of a foundation of hard work."

"ZFactor has proven to take professionals to new heights..."

The ZFactor is a powerful formula that has been proven to transform professionals and take them to new heights. I have seen "Product Sales Professionals" follow the formula and allow it to completely change their lives in just 36 months. Both their business and their customer lifetime value increased dramatically, while they became proactive in managing their customer relationships.

So I have a charge for you: go nurture your seed. Be disciplined in your execution, stay consistent and don't give up on your dreams. We have one life to live and there is no reason you can't redefine your future. Fight your demons, stay focused and go grow that big ass olive tree!

Be Boundless!

Jason A. Black
CEO, Founder
Boundless Network, Inc.
August 2012

Preface

A Revival of Authentic Sales Professionals

by Alan W. Goldsberry

A renaissance in the sales profession has emerged during these challenging economic times. A renaissance is a time of rebirth or revival of culture and skills that have been forgotten or previously ignored. Conventional wisdom for the *tricks-of-the-trade* salesperson is being replaced by the highly experienced, knowledgeable, and skillful *sales professional* who has mastered the art of sales and made it a sustainable, scalable process. In fact, top producers are learning basic coaching skills to better serve their clients.

A traditional salesperson bemoans their situation and keeps searching for the magic bullet, a new technique or trick to make a sale. Whereas the seasoned sales professional steps back from the situation as a sculptor when viewing a block of granite. The authentic artist does not see the block of stone. The artist sees the beauty waiting to be revealed from within. Then, and only then, do they begin chipping away the obstructions that hide the best of the stone, from within.

> Successful sales professionals desire to coach and mentor emerging sales professionals.

This rapidly expanding movement is transforming long held sales traditions into a revival culture of professionals who are experts in their respective field and focused on coaching clients toward unique, tailored solutions that create significant value for clients. They are supercharging performance by leveraging technology and coaching with the proven attitudes and aptitudes of historically successful sales professionals.

In reality, this is not news to any authentic, successful professional. What is news is how these authentic individuals are now speaking out. Their commentary is not about *how they achieved their success* but *how you achieve your success* and they are willing to be a coach or mentor for emerging professionals. It is not a *look-at-me* and *how I did it*—it's about coaching and mentoring others on how to think, act and sell differently to leverage and mold time-tested best practices and defining characteristics to

You will experience an acceleration of your sales results and increase in performance with ZFactor.

fit with your unique gifts, talents, experience and situation. It's about your sustainable success, not their fifteen minutes of fame. These professionals know how to create value and desire to make a difference with other sales professionals and inspire them to discover their own pathway to success.

And, I happen to be married to one of the best and most authentic sales professionals on the planet and author of this book. Of course, I'm biased, and I encourage you see what others have had to say about working with her by checking out the recommendations published on her LinkedIn. http://www.linkedin.com/in/cgoldsberry.

Cindy, as a thought leader in the sales profession, has leveraged her deep understanding of the sales process and embraced the rapidly evolving landscape of today's sales environment to establish effective strategies, resulting in significant and sustainable value for clients, sales professionals and employees. One of these strategies is how she has customized the ZFactor methodology to contain the best of her experience and knowledge along with that of other proven, successful sales professionals and business builders. This book is a collaborative effort with the mission to reveal and release the untapped potential in those professionals who desire to be authentic, value creators for their clients and achieve greater success.

With nearly 30 years of sales experience, Cindy brings a unique and distinct voice with a deep understanding of the sales process and wisdom to know the challenges of the sales vocation from both a producer and sales leader's role. She knows how to drive sales performance, yet maintain a best practices integrity and authenticity from both a business-focus and client-first perspective. She has the credibility of being an early addition to the executive team of Boundless Network, Inc, an Austin Ventures company. She joined the company in 2006 when there were 11 sales professionals and annual revenues of $1MM and as of publication date, there are 150 sales professionals with $43MM in 2011 sales.

Cindy asked me to provide a brief overview of the origins of ZFactor, as I am the creator and developer of the methodology. A brief overview is here with additional detail in the Appendix, entitled the Thinking Framework.

Origins of ZFactor

For some thirty-five years, ZFactor has been a gift that keeps on giving, and it is in the last fifteen years that the concepts behind ZFactor have evolved into the formal methodology that you see today. There are a few defining moments and discoveries, but the vast majority of ZFactor has been an evolution over the years of thoughts and ideas, people, processes and technology, implementation and metrics, all in a state of continuous review and refinement.

There have been hundreds of people and thousands of interactions engaging with others in discovering and exploring the power of skillful thinking with ZFactor or one of its earlier versions. Yet, skillful thinking, on its own will not make something happen. One can take on their best *The Thinker* (the statue) pose and be in deep internal thought and wish for change, but success only becomes possible for those who put thoughts into action.

During my entrepreneurial and advisory career, there have been extensive interactions with many different people, in all types of situations and various industries. As my roles evolved into leading and developing others, it became clear that skillful thinking does not come naturally for humans. It is a learned skilled and must be continually practiced and improved. The challenge is in how to encourage other people to think differently about what they do in ways that motivates them to reveal and release untapped potential. Most importantly, the objective is to find the most powerful way to align the thinking of all parties, so that discussion, plans and actions can swiftly result in producing results.

I've been involved in multiple fast growth opportunities. Extensive training and long term mentoring is not possible during fast growth. Encounters and interactions are brief, at best. Everyone is unique with very different backgrounds with very different personal and professional agendas. So then, how does one step away from the chaos and *herding the cats mentality* and truly find a powerful process to get others on the same page and moving in the same direction in the shortest amount of time?

From a simple formula in 1984 to this book, ZFactor has evolved through many different names, iterations and technology applications implemented in

ZFactor Sales Accelerator... an easy to understand and easy to use process to close the gap between where you are and where you want to be.

This book really is your *Pathway to Success* if you believe and desire to achieve similar successes revealed within.

a variety of industries, roles and situations. There are multiple applications and books that will be brought to market and in a variety of industries over the next few years, all using the foundational ZFactor methodology, including the K.A.R.T.E Formula, Success IQ, Investor IQ and Executive Financial Value Predictor.

This is the second book in the sales acceleration series. The first book focused on life insurance sales and this book focuses on product-oriented sales. Additional books in development in the sales acceleration series will focus on sales management, financial services, real estate, professional services and customer service. Other ZFactor series of books will be developed for leadership, management, mentoring, coaching and advisory. I am constantly on the look-out for the right expert with the right skills to take on writing another ZFactor book.

If interested in learning more about writing a ZFactor book, go to the website www.zfactorgroup.com. At this website, you can also learn about implementing ZFactor into your organization and becoming certified to train and coach the ZFactor methodology.

This book really is your *Pathway to Success* if you believe and desire to achieve similar successes revealed within. This book has been adapted with a customized ZFactor methodology to fit you. You will be challenged and, of course, change has its pains and gains. Yet, when one knows what to do and how to do it and then employs the defining characteristics of successful people, the pain can be minimized and gains accelerated. So sit forward and put on your thinking cap to enjoy the stories Cindy shares that can give you a peek into what's possible for your success. Then make a plan and take action to chip away those mental obstructions to realize the untapped potential within you.

May you be challenged beyond your current beliefs and achieve greater success than you ever imagined.

Alan W. Goldsberry, CEO, Author, Creator of ZFactor
Austin, Texas
August 2012

Guide to Book

Accelerate Sales and
Build a Sustainable Business

Reveal and Release Untapped Potential

Thank you for spending your valuable time to read this book. Many of us have questions about sales, business development and work-life balance. While the content will answer some of those questions, you will discover how a simple, yet powerful *XY* graph and ZFactor methodology will empower new thinking and reveal and release untapped potential for greater success.

Meet the Author—Cindy G. Goldsberry *(quick view)*

- 30 year career—28 years in sales and sales leadership.
- Background: Computer Sales, Big 4 consultant, Entrepreneur, Sales Executive, Coach, Mentor, Advisor, Church and Community Leader.
- Track record of successful sales team and revenue development in fast growth companies.
- Bio and Sales Autobiography in back of the book.

Who should read the book?

- Sales professionals who sell products and product-oriented services, with the opportunity to build a business.
- Sales Professionals interested in being treated as a business partner, not just as a vendor.
- Sales executives and managers: develop coaching managers for more sustainable sales performance. Companion book for managers available by end of 2012.

Reservoir of Tools, Ideas, Concepts, Defining Characteristics

All strategies and information described in book have been used and proven effective by the Author and collaborators, who are top producers and successful business builders.

This book is for anyone who wants to accelerate sales performance and build a sustainable business.

ZFactor makes your current sales system work better and helps you focus your development activities to improve sales skills and best business practices.

What do you do when work and life throw you a challenge or want to limit you?

It's not what happens to you, it's how you respond.

Key Points of Book

- ZFactor is a sales map.
- A new thinking tool.
- Successful people think and act differently.
- Gaps exist between your current perform-ance and your goals.
- Identify and quickly cross those gaps.
- Defining characteristics of top producers are revealed.
- Apply the defining characteristics to drive your success.
- Be strategically important and hard to replace.
- Become a Value Creator.

Top Producers Think, Act and Sell Differently

This book reveals how top producers learn to think, act and sell differ-ently. That's right. Every top producer has to learn how to think differently about who they are, how they think, how they do what they do and how they are going to become successful. It's a journey that requires your full atten-tion, focus and intention. The book shows the roadmap. Then, it's up to you.

Roadmap—From Vendor to Value Creator

The ZFactor methodology has been customized to provide you with the essentials for transforming your business from being a vendor (always being *bid-out*) to becoming a recognized expert as a Value Creator—establishing a successful, sustainable business. The process, pathway, strategies and defining characteristics are shared from experiences by the Author and from relationships with top producers over decades of sales success.

A Sales Map for Business Growth—Make it Fit your Unique Situation

When planning a trip, some will do extreme planning while others just jump in the car and go. You will find the concepts and information in this book adaptable to any professional situation or sales style.

When you work through this book from front to back, you will gain some amazing insights about yourself and your business that will accelerate your sales performance. If you are the type of reader who likes to hop around the book, you will gain some acceleration, but you may miss out on some key development opportunities that could improve performance even more. If you do nothing else, take the assessment, in Chapter 2.2, and review the Defining Characteristics in the corresponding section in Chapter 3.

The Story of Pat and Terry

A story unfolds throughout the book as two main characters meet in the North Side Coffee Shop to discuss their professional situation and realiza-tions as they consider the concepts of *ZFactor Sales Accelerator*. The Author offers this story to help readers gain a better grasp of the concepts and how to put the ideas and practices of top producers into daily practice. While the names are masculine, we trust you to realize the characters can be male or female.

Pat is an average sales producer, and his mentor, Terry is a top producer. The story begins in a local coffee shop, where Pat realizes he is in another sales slump, yet something is different about this lack of momentum over prior times. He wonders about what to do and briefly considers he may be in the wrong profession. Terry arrives at the coffee shop and their conversation turns to this new book Terry has just reviewed for a dear friend and mentor. They openly discuss Pat's situation, challenges, opportunities and revelations within the context of the new book.

You may feel as if you are sitting at a nearby table and overhear this conversation as it clearly develops into mentoring sessions. You have a unique opportunity to glean a few insights for yourself as you pick up some tips to put into action relative to your situation. Pat goes on to achieve his goals because of his desire and willingness to invest his time into using the *ZFactor* concepts and practices.

The Author sincerely believes you will find parallels between your own situation and the story. The story is an amalgamation of actual encounters as a sales professional and sales leader. You are encouraged to grab a cup of coffee or tea, take a seat at your local coffee shop and imagine you are sitting at a nearby table next to Pat and Terry. Enjoy the story AND take the opportunity to reflect upon how Pat's situation may relate to you. Be willing to engage and most importantly answer the **Ask Yourself** questions and make note of the things you think about as you read. The sidebars are provided as a place for you to put your notes. Also record your *Unanswered Questions* and how you plan to get the answers you need to move you forward.

A unique aspect of this book is how it is written from the perspective of top producers. Rather than telling you how they, the AuthorI or anyone else specifically achieved success in a *How To* format, the essence of success is conveyed, which is to think and act differently. Be on the lookout for moments of insight for new ideas that you can adapt to your unique situation to accelerate your sales. No matter what, HAVE FUN!

Part One—A New Thinking Tool for Success

A new thinking tool is presented—(a simple *XY* graph) that guides you to think and act like a top producer. The concept of becoming a *Value Creator* gets introduced and how *ZFactor Self-Coaching* process empowers the Five Essential Disciplines of Top Producers that can change thinking and results.

Adopt the courage and Spirit of the Warrior!

"People who are successful at anything, are people who take action once they know what to do and how to do it."

Ackerman's Law of Success

Thomas E. Ackerman: Co-Author of ZFactor Sales Accelerator for Insurance Professionals

Part Two—The ZFactor Sales Accelerator

Takes a look at the *ZFactor Sales Accelerator* methodology and how Pat used it to get out of his sales slump and begin building a sustainable business. A unique and simple self-assessment helps you to clarify where you are as it relates to your sales growth and putting a plan of action in place to get to where you want to be.

Remember why you first started doing what you do. Imagine bigger possibilities and keep on keeping on.

Part Three—Defining Characteristics of Top Producers

Defining Characteristics of Top Producers are presented as a pathway to success. Learn how to establish a plan to bridge or cross the gap between reality and potential. Change can be an adventure and exciting when you know where you are, where you want to be and how to get there.

Part Four—The ZFactor Butterfly Effect

Stuff happens. As a sales professional, when you understand and apply the ZFactor Butterfly Effect, you are in a unique position to make a significant impact for clients. As you fully embrace how the work you do creates meaningful value for others you will experience a sense of purpose and meaning to be enjoyed and celebrated.

Part Five—Concluding Thoughts

Concluding thoughts and the 30 Day Challenge.

PART ONE

THE (Z) FACTOR

NEW THINKING TOOL FOR SUCCESS

Chapter 1.1

A New Thinking Tool for Success

Pat looks out the window of the North Side Coffee Shop, watching the rain. Shaking his head, he looks at his watch to see that it is ten minutes after the hour. He mumbles to himself, "I should have held this meeting at her office." But, Pat didn't want to drive all the way downtown and mess with carrying his portfolio and samples, so his prospect agreed to meet at the coffee shop on the way into work. Just then, Pat's phone chimes with a new text message. Sure enough, the prospect explains she has a conflict and will not make the meeting. Pat lets out a sigh under his breath, "Not again."

Imagine Pat's disappointment. He was looking forward to this meeting because it was his most recent and best opportunity to get into a company he had been targeting for months. Can you relate?

Pat is in the midst of a sales slump and needs to get new quotes going to get sales back on track. It was just a few months ago Pat was on his best sales streak. Hot and cold has been the norm since he came into the business. While disappointed, he begins to reflect on his sales activities over the past few weeks. Sales practices have been less consistent and the daily routine feels stale. Something needs to change, but what? Pat takes a little time to reflect on current activities and decides to use the next hour to come up with some new ways to increase sales.

> Pat is disappointed with his current sales production.

As Pat sits deep in thought, Terry, a friend and mentor, comes into the coffee shop. Terry sees Pat and figures he must be sending or reading a text. He guesses Pat must not be expecting anyone or he would have looked up when the door opened. Terry selects a juice and walks over to say hello.

"Good morning, Pat." As Pat glances up Terry immediately recognizes a touch of disappointment on his face.

Pat is happy to see Terry. Maybe he has some good ideas to help Pat out of his sales slump.

"Oh, hey. Good morning, Terry. Good to see you. Would you like to sit down?"

"Sure, you bet. I've got a client coming in soon, so I've got a few minutes. What's up with you?"

As Terry sits down Pat thinks about the respect and honor he has for the friendship with Terry and how his mentorship has proven valuable through some challenging times for Pat. This feels like one of the more challenging times.

"I just had a good prospect cancel on me, at the last minute. She was referred to me by one of my best clients, and even agreed to meet with me after my first brief conversation with her. I was really hoping to show her some of my work, given a qualification call we had last week. Now, I'm sunk with her and disappointed. Cancelled meetings seem to be more the norm for me over the past few weeks. I need to get some quotes and make some sales soon."

"It doesn't sound like you lost the sale. It's just not happening today."

"Yeah, I know, but sometimes just getting in the door seems like it can take forever. I will follow up and reset the appointment."

"Pat, I've got about twenty minutes before my client arrives. Looks like you need to bounce around some ideas. Give me a quick update."

Find a mentor or a coach, who has proven success in the business. Ask them to work with you.

"Thanks, Terry. I really appreciate that. I'm really having a tough time getting my attitude on track. I just feel so worn out. Don't mean to be having a pity party here, but it seems like the stuff that always worked in the past isn't working anymore."

"Everything has seasons. This one might be winter for you Pat. But each season brings specific things that need to be done in preparation for the next. So...bring me up to date."

"Okay, it's been a few weeks since I've had any significant jobs to bid on. I hit a really good streak for a few months. It felt like everything I touched turned to gold. I know there will always be sales seasons and it seems sales are like bananas, they come in bunches, but something is very different about where I am this time. I'm not going to give up the ship, but sometimes I wonder if there might be a better career path for me."

"We all have those thoughts from time to time. It's only normal. And, it's okay to have the pity party for a few seconds, but then you have to move on. It's times like this that you have to fill the void with the right people and information to keep you on track. You know me, I'm always curious about new concepts and ideas and I love to learn as much as I can about getting better at sales and improving my knowledge about this business. Over the last several months I have been really working on moving away from being just another vendor selling product to understanding how I can improve my abilities and create sustainable value for my clients."

"That's nice to think about, but I just need something to help me make some real sales—and quick."

"I got it. But hear me out. A few months ago, a good friend invited me to preview a book she wrote. She's had a twenty-eight year career in sales and marketing and has adapted a sales methodology developed by her husband for our industry. It's called, *ZFactor Sales Accelerator: From Vendor to Value Creator for the Product-Oriented Sales Professional*. I've realized that it is *so* easy to get stuck in *vendor mentality* and find yourself living the grind of existence from one order to the next order. But the premise of this is that successful people think and act differently. Sounds really simple, but when was the last time you tried to change the way you think?"

"Terry, I was just considering that before you walked over. I'm ready to make some changes, yet I'm stuck thinking about how I've gotten here once again. Actually, I'm tired of this up and down with my sales. I am really tired of the work that goes into quote after quote only to be out-bid or trumped by a prior relationship. I've always pulled myself out of slumps before, but something feels different this time. I'm not sure what to do. So, what's different about this book? I don't need another rah-rah, feel good book, sales training system, podcast on the ten steps to success or a premise on how to get the secret ingredient in my life right now."

Terry chuckled. "Believe me – it's not a magic pill, nothing is, but it will give you food for thought. This ZFactor method takes a much different approach to selling. The objective is to help professionals build sustainable and repeatable business, which means greater ROI on the time invested in each and every sale. Instead of telling you how *others* are successful, the

> Terry is focused on moving away from just being another vendor (tired of always in bidding situations) to becoming a value creator.

book encourages you to think through how to maximize your *own* strengths and skills to make your business successful.

Terry encourages Pat to consider thinking differently about his business.

"Instead of *How To* tactics, the book gives you the thinking strategies and defining characteristics of successful sales professionals. It encourages you to reflect on how you think about success, what you think about and the actions you need to take. Then it provides self-coaching tools and templates to guide you and keep you accountable. Once you understand the basics of the ZFactor method, you realize how it can be an effective tool for always knowing where you are in your business, how to relate to your current and prospective customers, and what it takes to build a successful business."

"Sounds like something I'll be interested in when I get myself out of my current slump. Right now, I need to find more prospects."

"I'm sure you do. But do you really know where to look for them? Given what you've said, Pat, I believe now is the perfect time for you to try this out. Believe me—I do understand your situation and you have to do what works for you—and of course continue to do what it takes to put bread on the table. But if you started today and began changing little by little what you did every day...in 6 months the results can be significantly different than today. Wouldn't that mean something for you? I think it really could help you start on a more sustainable trek—versus the up and down road you've been traveling."

"You really believe that?"

"Yes I do. If I had this ZFactor methodology twenty years ago, I believe it would have made an incredible impact on by business today. I think there are some master sales professionals who get there naturally, but as you and I know, our industry has little to no training on offering value. Learning the features of your products or knowing how to ask questions or overcome objections is *not* offering value to the client. Or, for example, we can watch a master cold-caller pick up the phone and get someone on the line, but that doesn't mean ten other people could duplicate that! There is no such thing as a one-size-fits-all recipe for sales success. I'm more interested now in reflecting on the way I think about myself, this business, my strengths and what I'm passionate about to plan my approach to produce results. Would you like to see a quick little exercise on how to use ZFactor?"

"Terry, you are one of the most successful and creative professionals I know in this industry. Sure, I'll take the last few minutes you've got this morning to see what this is about."

"This will be fun. I've been looking for the right opportunity to share what I've been learning about ZFactor. This will help me gain more understanding for how it works, because I'll have to actually apply what I've learned so far."

"Well, you've always told me if I want to learn something fast, learn how to present the idea to others. So what's next?"

Terry pulls out the book and a single sheet of paper and lays them on the table. "You know, Pat, you aren't doing anything wrong. You already know something needs to change, and I know you. If you knew what to do, you would be doing it. This will help you get focused on what to do and how to take different actions to achieve better results."

"Well, you are already helping me get out of my down in the dumps thinking that has been getting the better of me."

"It's only natural for *stinkin thinkin'* to get the best of you. I have no doubt you will put yourself back on the track. If you want things to change…"

Pat quickly finishes the statement. "Then change the way you think, which will change the actions you take, and those actions will always produce different and better results. Not quite so eloquent a paraphrase from "*As a Man Thinketh*", but I think James Allen would be pleased! It looks like fate for you to come walking in today, of all days."

Terry cracks a little smile. "The entire methodology of the book is based on a powerful, but simple premise. Let me show you how a simple diagram on a single sheet of paper can help begin making these changes, right now. When I first was shown this, I was amazed how fast I got it." Terry pauses and then points to the paper.

At first glance, Pat sees two lines forming an *XY* graph, and the graph is split into quadrants. Each quadrant has a different title. Immediately, Pat notices a backward *Z* crisscrossing the quadrants that starts in the lower left hand quadrant. Terry explains this represents the four stages of development and performance of growing an independent sales-based business. The backward *Z* follows the natural progression of growing a sales-based

Sales Growth ZMap

Page 15 has a larger version of the Sales Growth ZMap. Page 16 has brief descriptions of each quadrant.

ZFactor helps you think how to organize sales activities to positively impact performance.

business from the lower left quadrant *Product Basics*, to the lower right quadrant *Preferred Status*, up to the upper left quadrant *Program Mastery*, and over to the upper right quadrant *Value Creator*.

Terry taps the page. "This diagram helps you to visually take note of where you are and where you want to be as a sales professional. The truth is, our experiences in sales are not linear, but are continually influenced by our circumstances. The methodology is designed to help you organize and focus sales activities to positively impact performance, based on where you and your customer are at this moment. It has captured the concept of thinking differently into a simple *XY* graph. You want to change your results, right?"

"Of course, I want to change my results. You and I have had some pretty extended discussions about this in the past. But it seems even when someone can see the benefit of making changes, they still resist or eventually stop making them."

Terry continues, "That's true for most people who try to make changes all on their own. Making lasting changes requires an environment of accountability and a continual evaluation of where we sit related to milestones we've established in our lives—personally or professionally. Ever lost weight or achieved a goal like running a 10K? Research shows when an individual receives support with the right tools and encouragement, they are more likely to make necessary changes and achieve established milestones.

"This *XY* graph is called a ZMap. It is a visual representation of the ZFactor sales acceleration methodology. This powerful thinking tool has been designed and customized for the professionals selling products to facilitate discovery of how to make those changes.

"Learning to think and act differently first requires self awareness as to who you are and how you think about what you do. ZMap helps you develop your self awareness and focus on performance improvement. Once you gain greater understanding for how ZFactor works, this almost becomes a one page book. It quickly stimulates you to focus on the right things to do at the right time with the right people. When ZMap is combined with the ZFactor coaching methodology you can accelerate your sales productivity to build a sustainable business."

A really simple way to change your thinking and accelerate success.

Terry pauses to take a sip of juice. Pat asks, "Okay, so what's next? I need to get something going."

"I understand. Think of this as a simple road map showing you where you are and what to do to get where you want to be. This is your journey... your map. In the past, I would listen to what others did to make them successful and try to duplicate what they did. That seldom worked, because I would find out they had some skill or resource I didn't have. Maybe, it was experience, knowledge or access to certain resources."

"Terry, can you give me an example of what you are talking about?"

"Sure. I once heard a guy say his success was because he did two presentations a day, three days a week to business owners. So, I started cold calling or walking into small businesses trying to get appointments. After a couple of weeks, it was clear it wasn't working for me. I didn't have the right knowledge, skills, network or experience to even qualify the prospects. The truth is, I abhorred having to try and sell to someone cold like that. But like you, I needed to make a sale and so I was trying to do something different. My manager kept encouraging me to get out there and knock on more doors.

"Finally, one of the older guys in the office took me to coffee and suggested I take some time to think about my network and who might refer me to companies that are a good fit for me. He also said I needed to learn more about specific products and clients that would have an interest in those products. Then, develop some additional sales skills before I could be successful selling to interested decision makers. While I didn't realize it at the time, that coffee shop experience put me on the pathway to building the successful sales system I have today. This has helped me focus on who I am, my strengths, skills and resources. That's why I say, I wish I had this book twenty years ago. It would have saved me a lot of time and heartache!"

"Okay. Sounds like you might be telling me to stop looking for a magic pill to try and increase sales. Oh yeah, you did say that, didn't you?"

"Pat, we all have to learn this at some point. If you don't learn this, the option is going from sales slump to sales streak and back for the rest of your career. The key is first, knowing what to do...based on who you are. *Sales acceleration happens when you learn how to adapt knowledge of who you*

Sales Growth ZMap

Program Mastery	Value Creator
Map Your Pathway to Success	
Product Basics	Preferred Status

Page 15 has a larger version of the Sales Growth ZMap. Page 16 has brief descriptions of each quadrant.

ZFactor is a useful tool to make coaching and management discussions more productive.

Sales Growth ZMap

```
                        Program Mastery  :  Value Creator

                        Map Your Pathway to Success

                        Product Basics   :  Preferred Status
```

are today to maximize the resources available to you to create momentum for change."

"So, ZFactor shows me how to do this?"

"Well, let's go to the ZMap and see. I could ask you a lot of questions and we could talk for hours about what holds back your sales performance and business growth. We might eventually get to something useful for you to take action on. ZFactor simply accelerates this process. It gets us on the same page quickly and keeps us on the same page to create a more productive outcome for you. What are your thoughts about this *XY* graph or ZMap in front of you?"

Pat pauses a moment to consider the graph. "Well, I see the natural progression in the growth of a typical sales business. What makes someone a *Value Creator*?"

"I had the same thought when I first looked at this graph. A Value Creator builds a sustainable business by attaining a base of customers with a predictable life-time value. This base, and the relationships therein, offer influence and momentum to create new opportunities to achieve even more significant results. I'm sure you've heard the phrase...*from success to significance*. That sums up the Value Creator. Clients and other professionals view them as a strategic partner who is continually offering value and deliver solutions that create value. A *Value Creator* is one who achieves the pinnacle of their career. While it takes time, the right stuff and specific results to be known as a Value Creator, you can learn to think and act like a Value Creator right *now*, if you truly desire this status."

Pat interrupts briefly, "So, you're saying there is a lot more to this *XY* graph than meets the eye. You called it a one page book. Guess you can't judge this one page book by its cover can you?"

Pat gets a laugh out of Terry. "Actually, I believe this has the potential to make management and coaching discussions more productive than the old standard methodologies. Improving sales performance is a complex process involving many distinct characteristics, people and situations. ZFactor simplifies this process and helps focus on what will increase sales today and build a solid business for the future. Let me ask you a question. With what you see on this page, where would you plot yourself on this graph?"

"Where would I plot myself? Do you mean to which quadrant do I relate?"

"Yes. Everyone has a starting point based on their past experiences. ZFactor helps you laser in on what you need to learn and do to bridge the gap between where you are and where you want to be. Taking a look at the labels on the quadrants, which quadrant best represents where you are, today?" Terry stops talking and sits quietly as Pat looks at the ZMap.

"I can't say I've achieved *Program Mastery* and I've been in the business long enough not to be in *Product Basics*. Although my attitude when you walked in today might indicate I'm in that quadrant. I guess the *Preferred Status* quadrant sounds more like where I am. I'm not real sure exactly what that means, but I do know I want to know more about the Value Creator quadrant."

Terry taps the ZMap. "That's all you need to get started moving in a new direction. The book provides a simple assessment to confirm where you plotted yourself. The book refers to this as your *Starting Quadrant*. Given this is where you are now, the next question to answer is where do you want to be or as the book refers to it—what is your *Target Quadrant*? All this gets explained in the book, by the way."

"I want to be the Value Creator. Would that be my target quadrant? This just looks logical since it's in the upper right and that's where the backward Z finishes."

"Eventually. From what I understand, to go from *Preferred Status* to *Value Creator* is a pretty big leap. You might not have it as your first target quadrant, but it is good to read and understand more about the Value Creator so you can apply those characteristics into your daily sales activities starting now. I think your *Target Quadrant* is *Program Mastery*, since it is the next quadrant on the backward Z. Now the fun begins. As you learn more about the ZFactor process and coaching methodology you will learn about the defining characteristics necessary to close the gap between where you are and where you want to be."

"Sounds good to me. Terry, what was your starting quadrant?"

Which quadrant do you see yourself achieving?

"I started in *Program Mastery* and have been moving toward *Value Creator*. There are several defining characteristics segmented into the quadrants that clearly describe what it takes to complete a quadrant and move forward to the next one. Based upon characteristics in *Program Mastery*, it appears I'm on track to achieve *Value Creator*, yet one doesn't really know they have become a *Value Creator* until they are acknowledged by clients as a strategic partner in the client's success. Basically, a Value Creator is much more than just a sales person or a vendor, because their clients are thankful for the value they have received.

"This is definitely not a book you pick up and read once. This book is more of a reference guide that continues to evolve as you do. I know you have lots of questions." Terry looks over Pat's shoulder. "And my client just walked in." Terry waves to his client who walks over to the table.

Terry turns to his client and says, "Henri, let me introduce you to Pat, a good friend in the business. Henri and Pat shake hands and acknowledge one another with a good morning greeting. Terry turns back to Pat and pushes the book and ZMap over to him. "I'll be 30 to 40 minutes. If you have the time, look at the ZMap and scan the book. Given all the hours we have spent together getting to know one another and each other's goals, values, strengths and weaknesses, consider what we could have learned in a fraction of the time with the ZMap. I'm going to be with Henri for about thirty minutes. She and I are just finalizing some of the elements of a program we've been working on."

"You bet. Thanks, Terry. I appreciate your time and thanks for sharing this with me. I look forward to learning more. Henri, nice to meet you. Terry is one of the most talented guys I know. You are fortunate to be working with him."

Henri nods. "Nice to meet you Pat. Yes, Terry is a great collaborator. He's really helped us get things in line and save us costs on this program. But he's been doing that for us for years. I don't know what we did before!"

Terry looks at Henri. "Thanks, that was nice of you to say."

Henri laughs. "You are welcome. Now let's go get this next program out the door, partner! What is this ZMap? Sounds interesting."

Ask Yourself

⇒ How many of your client's view you as strategic partner?

Terry begins walking away and turns back to Pat. "Pat, let me give you a question to ponder. How do you create value for your client's now? See you in a bit."

Pat takes a moment to watch Terry and Henri walk away and realizes Henri referred to Terry as her partner for specific business initiatives. Given what Terry just said about the Value Creator, it certainly appears Terry got confirmation he creates value for his clients. "Wow," Pat whispers to himself.

Pat looks back at ZFactor and realizes no one has ever handed him a simple roadmap for his business as a product-oriented sales professional. Constantly being bid out, having to shave margins and compete on features and functions have all taken their toll over the years. Pat begins to envision all the various pathways to choose from as he moves from being just another *vendor* to one who actually creates value for his clients. Amazing how a single sheet of paper and a little instruction can create so many questions and curiosity. How might he use this same concept to help his clients learn to re-think their relationships with him?

This on-going conversation *between Pat and Terry is a composite of many such similar events the Author has experienced personally, and with people mentored, coached and advised over the years. The ZMap has been used specifically in training and coaching product-oriented sales professionals in formal and informal settings and has also been used in a variety of situations, and adapted or customized to fit various careers and industries.*

Consider the book you are holding as a virtual Master Mind with the possibility to reveal and release your full potential to propel you forward and accelerate your success. Whatever you can imagine you want to know about becoming successful and accelerating your sales performance, is now available to you. Just in case you didn't catch it, let us help you grasp the premise of this book...

Successful people think, act and sell differently!

> This book becomes your virtual Master Mind to reveal and release untapped potential for success.

"People do not attract what they want, but what they are."

Ask Yourself

⇒ Who is attracted to you?

⇒ What situation dominates your thoughts these days?

Quotes from *As a Man Thinketh*, by James Allen first published in 1902.

"Men do not attract what they want, but what they are."

"A man is literally what he thinks, his character being the complete sum of all his thoughts."

> *"Mind is the Master power that moulds and makes,*
> *And Man is Mind, and evermore he takes*
> *The tool of Thought, and, shaping what he wills,*
> *Brings forth a thousand joys, a thousand ills: —*
> *He thinks in secret, and it comes to pass:*
> *Environment is but his looking-glass."*

Turn the page to view the full sized Sales Growth ZMap. Where would you plot yourself? As you read about the ways in which successful people think and act differently, keep the ***Ask Yourself*** questions in mind.

This is the Sales Growth ZMap Terry shows to Pat to start him thinking differently about his situation. Given your knowledge, experience and skills, where would you plot yourself? Use the quadrant definitions on the facing page to give you a little more information about each quadrant.

Ask Yourself

⇒ Where would you plot yourself?

⇒ Where do you want to be?

⇒ What are your thoughts about who you have to be to get where you want to be?

Program Mastery   **Value Creator**

Map Your Pathway to Success

Product Basics   **Preferred Status**

Product Basics: You know who you are and what you sell. You are disciplined and competent with understanding of your available resources.

Preferred Status: You have integrated who you are into a consistent sales system and are continually improving. You have become a preferred vendor which increases your confidence to work with only your best and most profitable clients.

Program Mastery: You continue to invest into yourself and your business, especially as it relates to your presentation and communication skills. You are building a sustainable, successful business by delivering solutions for managing more complex client situations that have ongoing, predictable results.

Partner and Value Creator: You have achieved the pinnacle of your career marked by the fact that you and your acquired expertise are the differentiating factor, not your products. You have become both strategically important and hard to replace with your ideal, favorable clients. You bring all talents and resources to the client to collaborate, plan and deliver innovative results.

ZMap: Map Your Pathway to Success—A Summary of the Quadrants

1. **Product Basics for the Vendor:** Every journey has a definitive starting point and every professional has to know the basics about products, sales skills and business practices. One must have professional disciplines and good work habits to even have a chance to be successful. One might consider this the *Competence* quadrant, because the cornerstone for all success is competence related to your products and business model. You must know who you are, where you are, where you want to go and who you have to become to get where you want to be. This means a dedicated understanding to the resources available to you (people, process and technology).

2. **Preferred Vendor Status:** As the professional gains experience with clients, they learn to integrate who they are with their business practices to continue developing disciplines to support growth and repeatable business. Personal and professional knowledge, interests, values, experiences, and talents are developed into a consistent sales system, which is continually refined and improved throughout their career. Through this process, the professional establishes methods for attaining *preferred vendor status* (either formally or informally) and leverages these relationships to create a solid referral strategy that produces sustainable results. One can consider this the *Confidence* quadrant because the sales professional learns who the best clients are and implements strategies and consistent processes for acquiring and retaining their ideal clients. Here the client might say something like, "*I don't know what I would do without you.*"

3. **Program Mastery:** What separates the top producer from the average producer? The top producer continues to invest in learning and developing themselves personally and professionally. Everything they learned in Product Basics and Preferred Status now is applied to create the foundation for building a sustainable and successful business based on strategic business outcomes required by their clients. Here the focus is on integrating product and process solutions—and often communication strategies and technologies—into an approach that solves problems and

serves a specific strategic purpose. This quadrant is considered the *Communicator* quadrant, because relationships in the ideal client move from selling 1:1 to serving groups (buyer communities) or departments to deliver more complex results. Here the client might say something like, *"I don't know what we would do without you."*

4. **Partner and Value Creator:** The pinnacle of career success, the Value Creator no longer depends on their product to differentiate them with clients...*they* are the differentiating factor by providing a level of strategic value that is so interwoven into the fabric of the client's business that they are irreplaceable. A Value Creator has created a stable and sustainable business. They can project a lifetime value of their client base. They are the *Go To* expert and highly influential in the industry and local community. They are the role model others want to become because they have achieved a high level of financial success and a work-life balance of significance. The Value Creator is earned only when one experiences recognition of this status from others. For their clients, the Value Creator is known as the *Catalyzer* and they bring all their talents to the client to collaborate, plan and deliver on producing innovative results.

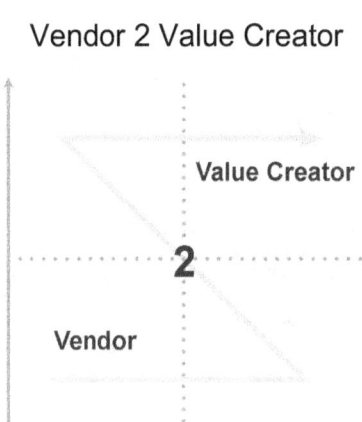

While every professional can learn to exhibit the characteristics of the Value Creator in every stage of their career, it is only when clients, other professionals and community leaders refer to and speak about the sales professional as a one who creates value—that the status is attained. Of course by then, the Value Creator doesn't care, because they are *others-focus* not *me-focused*. Becoming a Value Creator takes determined effort, intention, planning and time. Here the client might say something like, **"I don't know how we ever did it before you."**

Chapter 1.2

Successful People Think and Act Differently

Only you can make your dreams come true. Transform your thinking today and achieve your dreams.

Think and act differently. These few words sum up the premise of this book. When successful people speak—one hears the difference. When successful people take action—one witnesses much better results than the average. Successful people hear things differently, say things differently and do things differently. They have an integrity, faith, focus and frequency to their thoughts and actions that drive their beliefs, convictions, values, principles and practices. Who they are and where they are in life is the accumulation of experience, personal and professional self disciplines, and behaviors. One sees a demonstration of their character in how they conduct business and with their focus on serving and creating value for others. People feel listened to with them because their focus is on others, not on themselves.

You can absolutely change your results, your relationships and your life when you decide to change your thinking. When you change your thinking, your actions naturally change. Get on with it. You will be amazed at how simple it becomes to achieve dreams and make a difference for yourself, others and community.

One must think differently to chart a new and unique roadmap for success.

Start Thinking and Acting Differently Now

It takes practice, patience and perseverance to think and act differently. This is a skill you learn to continuously improve. Terry encouraged Pat to think differently when he pointed at the ZMap and asked, "Where are you?" Based solely on the quadrant titles *Program Basics, Preferred Status, Program Mastery* and *Partner—Value Creator*, Pat redirected his negative thoughts about his current situation to more productive thoughts.

He stopped thinking about being down in the dumps over a cancelled meeting. He was amazed at how simply choosing to think about where he is as it relates to building his business caused him to focus on what will help him make significant changes and grow his business.

Now, it's your turn. To change your thinking, right now, ask yourself a question or think about something other than what you were thinking about, right now. What happened? This will take practice.

How many times have you encountered a prospect (or even an existing customer) who does not understand the value you provide? Have you ever consider the value you provide? Or, considered how to present the value you provide to your clients? Are you ready to learn how to help them understand the value you provide and appreciate who you are as a Value Creator?

"The ancestor to every action is a thought."

~ Ralph Waldo Emerson ~

The world of product sales has changed vastly with the advent of technology and will continue to evolve toward more change, complexity and uncertainty. Often, your client has already done an Internet search and knows what they want, how much it costs and how long it will take to get it. If you stay stuck in old thinking and out-dated mindsets, clients will continue to think the way they think and push you into one of these categories:

- You will be considered as selling merely a commodity and thus your product has little differentiation. It's all about the price.

- Your products/services will be too expensive and you will be constantly put into bidding situations.

- Your client will want it "now" and when it takes too long for them to get what they want from you, they will go elsewhere.

You are unique. No one else can do what you do. ZFactor meets you where you are and can be customized to grow with you.

To become your client's strategic partner you must be a skillful thinker. Here are a few ways to practice and develop your thinking skills:

- Be curious about everything.

- Question to know and learn, never to judge.

- Challenge yourself to focus on what's important in the moment to measure reality and reveal the truth.

- Explore new possibilities for the fun of it and build bigger dreams.

- Collaborate with others to craft the right solutions that make a difference.

- Be accountable to everyone.

> Be someone who creates significant value for others. The rewards are meaningful and substantial.

- Actively participate in a master mind or accountability group to reveal and release immense untapped potential and become a better person.

- Be intentional on understanding the whole picture and the whole situation so each tactical action is understood and moves things forward.

- Question personal beliefs until they become authentic convictions and values.

- Question conventional wisdom and myths to understand more deeply why things are the way they are…and how you can engage and contribute to enhancing the environment or situation (vs. passive or aggressive interaction).

- Reflect upon your experiences until you understand the lesson and blessing.

- Learn to hold two thoughts at the same time to reveal and release untapped potential. This thinking skill is used often with ZFactor. The *X* and *Y* axes of the *XY* graph are used to create a context for connecting developmental concepts. You will learn more about this later.

Are you ready to start thinking and acting like a top producer? Here's how Pat started on his journey...

Terry Returns from his Meeting with Henri

Terry returns and quickly asks as he sits down, "So, what have you been thinking about? How do you create value for your clients?"

"I'm thinking I've got a lot to think about and a lot of changes to make. I'm a little confused about where to get started."

"It can seem a little daunting. Let me ask you this. What is one thing different in your thinking since I left to meet with Henri?"

Pat takes a moment to gather his thoughts. Terry waits, knowing that when one asks a thought provoking question, it is time to be quiet and listen.

Ask Yourself

⇒ Have you ever considered how you create value and make a difference for clients?

"Well, now I realize I've never taken much time to think about how I create value for my clients, much less be thought of as a Value Creator. I do the basics for my clients—gather facts through questions, do my research, consider the specs for what they need and determine the best products for them. The results are based upon what the client decides to do—and if they approve of my pricing. I don't dig much deeper to understand my client or what they are really trying to accomplish—or even consider what would be of greater value to them. I focus on making the sale. That's how I get paid.

"This has made me aware I don't think much outside the box of just making the sale. I don't consider much else that might be going on with the client other than the immediate needs they have shared. I've gotten set in my ways and I'm always hoping to meet the prospects who need the products I'm offering. I'm typically only interested in learning more about my product offering when it proves of value for me to make another sale. Now I realize I need to spend more time thinking about creating solutions tailored to my clients' situations."

"Those are pretty honest comments, Pat. What do you plan to do with all this?"

"Well, after I heard Henri call you her business partner and say you have done more than just provide products, I realized I probably don't have any clients who think that of me, like that. I see now I need to think more about how combinations of products and a focus on what the client is challenged with will create a more valuable relationship with them. I know you handle complex solutions for your clients and you coordinate various service professionals to help manage client's unique situations. Wow, my head is swimming with all the ideas. I guess the single most important thought is I've got a lot to think about and learn in order to take my career to the next level. I must develop a deeper understanding about this business and learn how to do things much differently than I do them today."

"Yes, you do. Are you ready to take on a challenge like this? Most professionals want to but few are willing to do what it takes. It just looks like too much work for them. There is no way for you to learn everything fast enough to deal with your current sales slump, but you can start today making little changes that, over time, will establish a sustainable business. You can leave your sales slumps behind.

> Successful people live a life of purpose and meaning. This drives the actions they take today.

Successful people keep learning and growing. Their clients expect them to be the best at what they do.

Do what you have to do to be the best!

"Pat, it sounds like you have a taste for what's possible. Let me ask you a few questions to stir up some more thoughts. Have you ever seriously considered what your end goal might be for building your business? Have you ever written out why you have chosen to make this your career? Are the answers to these questions important to you?"

"Whoa, Terry! That's a whole lot more than I can think about right now. Those are all great questions. While I can come up with some general answers, I now understand each of those questions require some real thought and time to integrate into my daily work-life. I'm not sure I'm ready to even start trying to answer those until I take care of my current sales slump. You got me thinking about a lot of different questions and asking myself what I'm going to do next."

"Glad to hear it. You have to get your day-to-day disciplines and practices working for you again. You know all the simple things like call people, set appointments and get fact finding sessions, right?"

"Yeah, I just let myself get lazy. I know it's time to get back on track by doing the right things, at the right time with the right people."

"Good to hear you know it's just the basics that are the foundation for producing sales for you. I know you will do what it takes to persevere through all the changes and challenges. Let me encourage you to commit to better discipline in everything you do—especially in blocking time to think, plan and execute on the sales activities that will produce results. This should include both your personal and professional life. Then and only then will you achieve all the goals you can imagine for yourself in this career. It only takes a little discipline and planning."

"Planning is not one of my strengths."

"That's normal for most sales professionals. They desire to be more productive and have more, but they just keep going in reactive mode from day to day without ever taking time to think or plan what they need to do to increase sales. Many folks just act on what has come in the door rather than prioritizing what is before them so they can focus on the highest revenue generating activities first. Think about it...some of your projects make you a high hourly rate, while others can potentially even cost you money if you accounted for the time it took you to complete the sale! If you are at the whim and call of your customers and have no time management disciplines in place—your time is not your own. Planning is not something you do in a few minutes. And planning to become a Value Creator is much different than planning on how to get out of a sales slump."

"Okay, so why is planning so different for anyone who wants to be a Value Creator?"

"Great question. You will only learn by doing. It seems that successful professionals somehow figure out setting and achieving goals requires thoughtful, focused planning. Sounds funny, but you have to *plan to plan*. Everyone is told to do it. You know, plan your work and work your plan, but something has to click before you really get how and why it is so important. Believe me; successful people only do what works. For me, I had to do a lot of trial and error early in my career before I figured it out. ZFactor has even helped me gain more understanding why I need to further refine and improve my planning processes."

"Terry, this is a lot to absorb. I hear what you are saying and I'm still wondering what do I do now? Do I really have what it takes?"

"Well, deciding you do have what it takes is the key to you changing your results. You have to decide to do it, no matter what. Why not take a moment to review the ZMap again. You initially plotted yourself in the *Preferred Status* quadrant when I first showed it to you. Take a moment to re-read the descriptions on page 16 to see where you think you are on the ZMap, now."

Pat takes a moment to read the quadrant descriptions and looks up. "Well, based upon the way I've been talking this morning, it's pretty clear I don't have *Preferred Vendor Status* with my clients. I just jump when they call. I do have a lot of tools and techniques, but I haven't put those together into a consistent sales process nor disciplined sales practices. Hmmm...I guess I'm really in the *Product Basics* quadrant. After all the years in the business, that's a little depressing!"

"Well, you could be ignorant, keep fooling yourself and never change, or know where you are and plan your journey so you can get where you want to be! Don't judge where you are, because the truth is *even the Value Creator*

> Successful people do what has to be done to take care of clients.

has to continually revisit the basics to create continued success. What does the *Product Basics* description make you think about?"

"Honestly, after my last sales streak, I would have thought I graduated from the basics. I don't think I would have admitted that before now. I am amazed how quickly I am starting to actually think about what is missing. My typical process is to stay busy—often very reactive as you've said. But I guess in truth, I'm really drifting around, going through the motions until something good happens. Then I drop everything to tackle the thing that has come in the door. I don't really work a plan at all. The good thing about meeting with you is I'm beginning to see that this book will help me get on a pathway to follow. I've never had anything like this before. Wow. Talk about facing brutal facts. Am I the only one this bad off?"

"Of course not – no one is perfect or immune from the illusion that busy equals productivity or profit. Everyone goes through this process...including getting burned out after following the same drill year after year. It's normal. It's not just what you know or think—it's what you do with what you discover that makes all the difference. *Product Basics* appears to be the right place for you to start. Being honest with yourself will help you master this quickly. Take note of the description in this quadrant. Specifically, note where it says: know who you are, where you are, where you want to go, and who you have to become and leverage the resources needed to get there."

"That will give me a lot to think about. What do you recommend for getting started?"

"You have to learn to adapt your current skills and resources to your daily sales activities to adapt your attitude and behaviors for success. Think of it like a roadmap. Your destination is *Value Creator* and you are starting from *Product Basics*. Now, you begin planning your journey with your first milestone to be *Preferred Status*. The book offers exercises and defining characteristics of top producers to help you think through this process and put some plans in place."

"This is looking like a lot of work. What finally motivated you to commit to your business at his level?"

"Well, Pat, for me, it started when I had the opportunity to spend some time with one of our million dollar producers. I was at the annual sales

> It's not just what you know or think - it's what you do with what you know that makes the difference.

> Be wise in choosing friends, associates and environment. These will shape you. Choose the best and you will be the best.

meeting my first year with the company, and as I stepped into an elevator and the doors were closing, Nolen, one of the top producers for several years, stepped into the elevator while speaking with a friend. I didn't know him, personally, but I knew who he was because he was one of the key note speakers.

Nolen said to his friend, "Yes, this has been another good year, but you know what, I just feel like there is much more potential with my business than just placing orders to reach my financial projections. The huge projects end up being so much about price, logistics and middle men. It used to be fun, but now I just continue to have margin shaved from these orders, or worst, I am constantly on the lookout for being underbid. I need some inspiration."

"I was floored! How could he be bored with placing what I considered to be such large orders? After his friend got off the elevator, I asked a couple of questions and soon found myself outside the elevator having a discussion with Nolen. He asked about my business and experience in the industry. He was very encouraging and amazingly approachable.

"I asked him what he did to be so successful and Nolen surprised me again. He said that the main thing was to decide what I want my business to look like, know who I want to work with and why, and learn as much as possible about the people I plan to market my products to. He said most of his business came from personal introductions and that he was working on a plan to expand within a specific vertical market.

"I was surprised because I expected to hear something extraordinary. Instead, I heard common sense. I remarked on that and he went on to say that it starts with just the basics—organization and self-discipline. Then it came out once again, just like he said in his keynote speech: "Plan your work and work your plan." It seemed too simple. Surely there was more to being successful.

"Twice that following year, I received an email from Nolen, asking how I was and how my business was progressing. He even sent me congratulations on one of the larger sales I made. He became a distant mentor—and I didn't know it until recently, but Nolen actually participated in an early pilot of the ZFactor methodology several years ago. We continue to connect with each other at our annual conferences.

> Know what you want, who you want to work with and learn as much as possible about the people you plan to sell your products to.

> Be organized and be disciplined. Plan your work and work your plan.

> Use a little common sense. Know yourself, your clients and your resources and do it with a passion to make a difference.

"What I've learned over the next couple of years is that Nolen did transform his business, after almost leaving the industry entirely. You see, there comes a time when one's success does lead to a desire for more than money or status...it leads to a desire for significance. Nolen met with a variety of leaders in the industry and got some coaching and perspective for approaching his business in a new way. He pulled in personnel resources and used technology to help him change the nature of how he serviced his accounts. Now, looking at it, it's like he 'leap-frogged' into the Value Creator mentality once he decided to commit to this industry and his business with a mindset of creating value and significance. Today, Nolen might otherwise be saying he was tired of writing those large dollar orders...but I happen to know now that he's got a well-oiled enterprise program in place and an awesome team, so I doubt that! In fact, he enjoys knowing he has built a business that creates value for all his clients.

"Sometimes, Pat, we think there must be some secret ingredient to success. There really isn't. It is more likely hard work focused on a particular market with a passion to make a difference and create value for others. Nolen would tell you that and the mechanical things that must be done are the same for every top producer: "Plan your work and work your plan." When I realized what he meant...the very nature of my business changed."

"Okay, Terry. I'm going to follow your advice and dig into this book. I promise to do what it takes."

Keep people around you who support your ambitions. And, let these be people who challenge you to be great.

Change Your Thinking... Change Your Results...

This conversation between Pat and Terry is typical for a sales professional in a sales slump seeking better results. Did you notice any part of yourself in Pat or Terry—or Nolen? Successful people have a defining moment story similar to Terry's elevator moment. Will Pat's chance meeting with Terry in the coffee shop become Pat's defining moment story? The big question now—will Pat do what works? Or, will Pat slip back into the quest to find the Holy Grail of sales success and neglect to focus on the basics?

The common denominator in every defining moment story is how the moment changes the way people think about themselves and the way they do business. Every individual who has this sort of experience has the choice to take off on a personal journey to explore and discover essential and defining characteristics that work for them to create success. Some do. Most do not. What will you do?

We're going to leave Pat and Terry, for now, and pick up with them later. Over the next chapters, Pat will be focused on getting out of his sales slump. He plans to use the ZFactor Self Coaching process outlined in the next chapter to help him with planning and taking action. You can use this same process to lay the foundation for sustainable sales acceleration.

Pat wrestled with the challenge to think and act differently. It was clear he had to make the change and it's not easy to do. With Terry's encouragement, Pat looked back over the ZMap and read the quadrant descriptions on page 16. He did an honest self assessment and realized he should be focused on *Product Basics*.

Ask Yourself
⇒ Do you have a mentor?
⇒ If not, who would be a good mentor for you?
⇒ How will you invite them to work with you?

Ask Yourself

⇒ Where did you plot yourself?

⇒ How has this simple exercise helped you to think differently about who you are and what you do?

⇒ What becomes possible for you if you really begin to think and act like a successful person you admire and respect?

⇒ Do you have a mentor like Terry? If not, who could be a mentor for you? How would you invite them to be your mentor? If you do have a mentor, how can they support you to think and act differently?

⇒ Do you have a definite plan of action that you adhere to on a daily basis?

An effective coaching or accountability process converts a personal or professional desire, plan or dream into reality. Participation increases awareness about distinctions to assist a person's focus on specific actions to accelerate success. A coach encourages a discovery process to define your knowledge, attitude, behaviors, resources, experience and skills necessary to achieve goals. Investing time with a mentor, coach or as part of a Master

Mind group should be inspiring, yet keep you accountable to strategies and action plans developed. So, for getting you started on this journey, the *ZFactor Coaching Strategy* has been adapted to a self coaching process. With strong work habits, self-discipline and the *ZFactor Self Coaching Strategy* you can use the self coaching for yourself or as a guide to help you collaborate with a peer or within an accountability group.

Find someone to hold you accountable to your plans.

Chapter 1.3
ZFactor Self Coaching

Significant positive changes occur after you change the way you think and act. The impact of these changes accelerates relative to your level of engagement, intensity, faith, focus and frequency of activity. The more intense your engagement the faster performance improves. Too often people are not motivated to make changes until they get so frustrated with current results that they are forced to make changes.

Why do average sales professionals resist change? It's a basic human trait...*fear of an unknown* perception of the future. This fear of the unknown future causes them to be mired in a lack of self confidence, which holds them back and causes them to settle for mediocrity. On the surface, it seems easier or logical to just stick with what is known. The thinking is that if they keep doing what they know or are comfortable with, their future will somehow improve. Yet the truth is, the future requires *present* attention and intention for change to manifest. Even when someone knows a change today will make a better future, they still often lack the courage and fortitude to take appropriate actions to even find out what to do.

Successful people have always been willing to step into the unknown and make necessary changes. They know the achievements of today are a result of changes they made in the past. If the current course won't take you where you want to go, then changes must be made to get to where you want to be. It's just common sense. Learn what needs to change, make the changes and achieve greater satisfaction with results. Sustain these results by continually evolving your thoughts. Successful people have a distinctive *Warrior Spirit* that is willing to engage any uncertainty because they know this is how changes are made. They replace fear with confidence, courage and the will to do what is necessary to make something happen. They know

What **IF³**™ You Engage?

Intensity

X   Faith

X   Focus

X   Frequency

_____

Accelerated Success

The greatest compliment that was ever paid me was when one asked me what I thought, and attended to my answer."

~ Henry David Thoreau ~

when they face change with desire, intention and consistency this ultimately leads to a purpose-driven, meaningful life.

Managing Change is a Learned Skill and Competency

How is managing change a learned skill? People are creatures of habit and it is easier to stay with what one knows than to engage in what is unknown. It's easier to have the illusion of control and attempt to manage opportunity, but the greatest outcomes come from an inspired focus on what *could be* without the fear of what *might be*. Quite simply, this means the wherewithal and intention for doing something a new way, using a new technology tool, being brave enough to look foolish, enlisting a new resource, managing expectations and disappointments and learning from the failures and mistakes.

When the potential results are unknown, many often disregard exploring the uncharted path as an option. Learning to deal with the unknown, and manage the thoughts and actions as a result, makes you more competent in all things you choose to do. Competence leads to increased confidence. With confidence comes greater emotional capacity for managing change and dealing with the unknown. This then becomes a full cycle in personal development where capacity actually fuels momentum toward exploring new territory for the realization of new and expanded goals.

The way you thought and your beliefs as a teenager were most likely not as important or valid for you when you got into your twenties. Likewise, your thoughts and beliefs are different in your thirties from your twenties and so on. The values, experiences and goals change as we do and we must be willing to evolve thoughts and actions as we grow in age and experience.

When Pat got the text from his prospect cancelling the meeting, he immediately reacted by spiraling down with disappointment. He was initially only focused on his personal situation instead of considering the prospect's situation. Pat's emotional capacity was extremely limited because of how he was thinking about his lack of sales performance. He had only a limited amount of capacity for dealing with the prospect cancelling the meeting.

Consider this analogy. Before Pat and Terry got together in the coffee shop, Pat's emotional capacity for change would fit in a coffee cup. After time

"Fear always springs from ignorance."

"Do the thing you fear and the death of fear is certain."

~ Ralph Waldo Emerson ~

Ask Yourself

Change is good. You changed something to get you to where you are now.

⇒ To get to where you want to be, what do you have to change now?

with Terry and a commitment to invest time in personal development, Pat improved his thinking capabilities and increased his emotional capacity for managing change. Now, he has much more capacity for managing change and dealing with uncertainty.

The ZFactor proprietary methodology embraces this process of change by creating a path for making *managing change* a competency. As you gain awareness to personal thinking strategies you will notice distinctions and make choices that make you unique in your beliefs, values, behaviors and disciplines. This process requires intentional effort of time, exploration, taking risks and embracing uncertainty. The individual who learns to effectively think differently and manage change will always outperform the average.

As you engage in *ZFactor Self Coaching*, you will learn basic coaching strategies to empower and accelerate achievement of specific goals and objectives. You can use these basic coaching skills to coach yourself or help you get more out of the coaching process when you hire a coach or participate in an accountability group. If you manage a team and/or other sales people you can use this process to develop your coaching and management skills.

Remember to keep it simple. Ask yourself thought provoking questions to draw forth new thinking; take some time to reflect upon your answers to create a broader and deeper awareness; keep a journal; maintain a clear focus on specific actions; establish and execute your plan; and track your progress. The *ZFactor Self Coaching Strategy* and guidelines are included at the end of this chapter.

Reset Your Prospecting Mindset (Do a Reboot)

Everybody has a mindset, a habitual way of looking at or feeling about something. When someone says another person has *an attitude*, they are referring to some external evidence of a mindset, which shows up as some sort of behavior. This behavior can have positive or negative effects. Either way, the mindset can control the way you think and act and thus how others respond to you. A specific mindset can be so powerful that it stops you from doing exactly what is needed to drive success or it can be a power booster for success.

Ask Yourself

⇒ Do you resist change or embrace change?

⇒ Describe a time you resisted change and a time you embraced change.

⇒ What difference do you notice between the two?

Ask Yourself

Successful people are organized in how they think about their goals.

⇒ How could you use ZMap to help organize the way you think about your goals?

Ask Yourself

...thought provoking questions.

⇒ Reflect on your answers.

⇒ Keep a journal.

⇒ Maintain a clear focus on specific actions.

⇒ Establish and execute your plan.

⇒ Track your progress.

Your choice of attitudes, behaviors and interactions with others creates a mindset that will influence relationships and results obtained, even when you are not aware of it. This is why it is essential to make yourself aware of what you think and how you think—to get to know who you are. A normal thinking process is the sum of all sensory collected data, prior thoughts, decisions and experiences. All new information, ideas, situations and opportunities are filtered by all prior thoughts and experiences. A more developed self awareness can empower the formation of new opinions, values and belief systems to accelerate sales. The degree of your emotional response or reaction will greatly influence the resulting mindset. Your mindset is the driver of the choices you make and the actions and behaviors you exhibit in the external world.

Take a moment and ask yourself what mindset do you have about prospecting? Asking for referrals? Disciplining your time for revenue generating (not administrative) activities? Following up on clients you've not heard from in a while? Going the extra step on details? Is it a mindset that creates a strong desire to do whatever it takes? You want more prospects...more business? Change your mindset about prospecting and asking for referrals and start taking actions based upon that new mindset.

If you desire to advance your career and reach your potential, you must be committed to a continual evaluation of your thoughts so that they support the vision of the new you. Then ask yourself whether your thoughts are supporting your vision or holding you back? When you are aware of what is holding you back, you can reset (much like you would reboot a computer). After all, the mind is a computer. You can reboot it. All it takes is awareness and then time and attention.

Both/And Thinking - A Power Tool for Changing Thinking (the Reboot)

Either/Or thinking kills momentum and opportunity. In a sales situation when a prospect says something like "either I get the price I want or this discussion is over", it is clear you have little strategic value to that client. When a sales professional draws the proverbial line in the sand with a statement like, "either I get some traction on these outbound calls or I'm done for the week", then lost opportunity is not a theory, but a given. Developing your thinking skills prepares you for managing *Either/Or* statements others say to you and you say to yourself. How? Let's explore this more.

The opposite of *Either/Or* thinking *is Both/And* thinking. The practice of *Both/And* thinking takes the best of one concept and the best of an entirely different concept and brings them together to create alternatives and new possibilities for success. *Both/And* thinking is essential for evolving who you are as a sales professional. You must be willing to question your current mindset, your values, behaviors and beliefs about your sales disciplines and business practices to accelerate your success.

Both/And thinking starts with a question. It is a simple methodology that considers two options *AND* multiple outcomes. This *possibility thinking* can quickly reveal and release untapped, unseen and unknown potential. Conversely *Either/Or* thinking starts with a declaratory statement, which clearly demonstrates a specific opinion, belief or attitude and most often with the expectation of a fixed or rigid outcome. Which do you think works better in a sales situation? Throughout the book there are *Ask Yourself* questions and exercises to help you compare your thinking to the defining characteristics of successful sales professionals. These questions and exercises are designed to encourage *Both/And* thinking. You are challenged to consider *Both* how you are similar to the top producer *AND* how you are different. The objective is for you to discover how to adapt and apply the defining characteristics to fit your strengths and skills.

What is a change you want to make in your thinking?

When Pat's client cancelled the meeting, Pat got frustrated and thought he missed an opportunity to develop a new client and closed his mind to any other options. Terry's comment *"sounds like you didn't lose the opportunity; it's just not going to happen today",* offered Pat a different perspective and gave him reason to do *Both/And* thinking. Rather than continue to think the sales opportunity was lost, he realized he had alternatives. In this case, Pat could set a new appointment for another day.

A true sales professional knows who they are. They have clearly defined convictions, beliefs and values especially as it relates to sales disciplines and business practices. This is important because you need to know which

Top Producers use *Both/And* Thinking

A top producer welcomes and engages everyone they meet. They don't make snap judgments *AND* they are clear about who fits their ideal client profile. They always make others feel good about who they are, even if not an ideal client.

Average Producers are more likely to use *Either/Or* Thinking.

An average producer seldom has an ideal client profile, so they hope everyone is a possible client. They waste a lot of time trying to find out if someone is *EITHER* a client *OR* not. Sadly, they begin to make snap judgments about people and miss out on opportunities to be referred to potential clients. People they meet also think *EITHER* I'll refer them or *NOT*. More likely *NOT!*

"The test of a first rate intelligence is the ability to hold two opposed ideas in mind at the same time and still retain the ability to function."

~ F. Scott Fitzgerald ~

battles you are willing to fight, no matter what. It is just as important for you to be willing to question your beliefs and values to uncover old, outdated or inappropriate beliefs and thoughts you realize are holding you back from achieving your goals.

If you want your career to accelerate, then develop *Both/And* thinking and use it in all aspects of your work-life. This thinking strategy will help you avoid becoming opinionated and overly involved in the type of discussions that kill sales opportunities. You will find *Both/And* thinking will make you a better person, more productive and happier.

The goal is to cultivate and nurture a new mindset for thinking about how to create value for your clients. Soon we'll explore specific disciplines of Top Producers to help you evaluate where your focus should be and what gaps might be holding you back from accomplishing goals. As you read through these be especially aware of your thoughts. Remember the current success you have or lack thereof, is the result of your thoughts and actions in the past. You are what you think about and what you do. Change your thinking, make better choices, take different actions and get better results.

Pat Starts Self Coaching

Pat realizes he needs to change his old mindset if he wants success like Terry's. He has to make some significant changes in his thoughts, attitude and behaviors. Even with Terry's mentorship, Pat decides to use *ZFactor Self Coaching* because he has to this point put very few disciplines in place to help in accelerating his success. He remains confident about his current sales skills yet realizes his self-disciplines and work habits have to be stronger. Pat has begun keeping a journal, which is a powerful tool for observing the evolution of personal and professional development. Here is an excerpt from Pat's journal.

Excerpt from Pat's Journal

When I first started in this business, I had good work habits and self-discipline. I see now when my level of sales results increased—I became reactive—and instead of adjusting my disciplines and habits to fit the new activity, I stopped doing what was working and went into a 100% tactical and reactionary mode. I see now how this led to getting so fixated on making a sale, I got absorbed in the details and let myself go into survival mode. This became so self-absorbing I dropped doing any forward looking planning. Initially, there was good momentum and sales were good. This lulled me into thinking that would just continue to happen. I even began to assume my new clients would know I needed referrals without me having to ask them. Things were going so well I stopped asking for referrals. I know referrals don't just happen. It takes diligent and consistent effort and I need to always ask. It's really clear I must be intentional and focused on evolving my mindset and establish the right habits and disciplines to match the level of success I want. Terry makes it all seem so effortless and I know he has had his challenges. I also realize I can't do it the way he does it, but I can match the intensity he has for serving his clients and achieving goals. I am committed to working through ZFactor.

Five Disciplines of Top Producers

Pat moves on to review and reflect on the Five Characteristics of Top Producers. He compares personal thoughts, actions and results to these characteristics and makes notes in his journal as to which ones are solid strengths and which ones require development. After you review and reflect on these characteristics, as Pat has done, you are encouraged to complete the **Self Coaching Reality Check** on page 43.

How do you compare with the characteristics on the following pages? Which are solid strengths for you and which ones need attention and action to create solid disciplines and practices? As with all the questions and areas of reflection in this book, it is suggested you take out your journal and write the answers, thoughts and questions that come up as you reflect on the content.

Five Disciplines starts on next page.

Manage Change

- Increased capacity will increase confidence.

- Increased confidence will increase courage to release your warrior spirit to reach higher and achieve your goals.

As you have new thoughts, take time to organize your thoughts into one of three buckets.

- Something you can do now;

- Something to do later;

- Not something you plan to do.

<table>
<tr><td>

Ask Yourself

What changes need to be made in the areas listed below to improve the odds of you achieving your goals?

⇒ Abilities:

⇒ Associates:

⇒ Behaviors:

⇒ Community:

⇒ Emotions:

⇒ Exercise:

⇒ Family:

⇒ Finances:

⇒ Friends:

⇒ Hobbies:

⇒ Skills:

⇒ Time:

</td></tr>
</table>

1. **Reflect on Basic Practices and Disciplines:** A top producer questions and reflects upon all their thoughts, actions and results related to sales activities, time management, disciplines, behavior, performance, quality of service and value to clients. The question most top of mind—*"Is this making me money and producing value for my business?"* If it is, they learn to maximize that activity. If it isn't, they stop it, immediately.

Ask Yourself

⇒ How would I rate my ability to maximize productive basic practices and sales disciplines?

These would be areas such as planning, time management, managing distractions, etc. Think of a basic practice or sales discipline and give yourself an "A, B, or C". A is the best.

2. **Keep a To Do List, Stop Do and Who Do List:** This characteristic can improve sales productivity in a matter of days.

Ask Yourself

⇒ What activities, behaviors, disciplines and practices do I need to start doing and which ones must I stop doing?

⇒ What am I best at (keep doing) and what is not a good use of my time (so I can stop doing or outsource the activity)? What activities am I doing that must be done, but someone else can do?

3. **Invest in Personal and Professional Development (your own money and time):** Top producers love learning new things especially when it makes more money and serves clients. They are curious about a wide assortment of things and love to know more about people and under-stand what makes people think and do what they do. Top producers always have a special interest in their business as a whole and will invest in talent and process oriented resources to move the needle. As a result of their passion and ability to develop such a deep understanding of their business, others enjoy for them to share what they know. They don't follow the pack and do things just because everyone else is doing

them. In fact, others do what the Top Producer does. The key here is they invest in themselves because they love to and it produces value for their clients and those who work with them. If they don't enjoy what they are doing and it doesn't produce value, they stop doing it and/or invest in other resources to take it on.

Ask Yourself

⇒ When and what was my last investment in personal or professional development and/or for growing my business?

⇒ Do I MAKE the time to set goals, review my plan, write in my journal…reflect? If not, what will it take to do so?

⇒ Do I devote a specific percentage of my earnings to investing in personal and professional growth and development?

⇒ What's something I know about or do that others want to know more about?

⇒ What makes me special?

4. **Have a Make It Happen Attitude (goal and achievement oriented):** You feel this attitude exuding from top producers. They think and act very differently from average producers. Some might call it confidence or positive attitude. It goes much deeper than either of those or any label one might give. This attitude comes from the core of who they are. They are not born with it. One might say it has been a burning ember with them always and thus has become a learned skill with intentional development over a period of time. It has taken intense focus and investment to understand who they are, their values and beliefs. Attitude drives *Aptitude* for these people. This understanding gives them the confidence and courage to pursue opportunities and make things happen. This process helps them learn how to deal with the unknown and manage change. They know themselves, their clients and how to leverage resources to make things happen for themselves and others. They don't bemoan *what is* but embrace *what can and/or must be*. They learn these things by being intently aware of all they experience including failure

Ask Yourself

⇒ Do all your daily actions make money or produce value for your clients?

and success. They have learned how to maximize the right actions with the right people at the right time.

Decide to make it happen and then practice, practice, practice… and keep at it until it happens!

Ask Yourself

⇒ How intensely do I think about my strategies for what is next with my largest opportunities?

⇒ How intensely do I pursue revenue producing relationships?

⇒ Do I have written plans and know how and when to adapt my plans to achieve greater success?

⇒ Do I set aside time to plan my work and then evaluate the work done to plan each and every week?

⇒ Is my plan so ingrained in me that I am aware of new opportunities when they present themselves?

⇒ Am I truly committed to do what works to make something happen in each instance?

Expect a coach to be a good listener, results oriented, part sounding board, task-master, strategic advisor with expertise in your industry and a genuine cheerleader.

5. **Be Willing To Do What Works and STOP what doesn't. (appropriate and produces value):**   You have to get real with yourself. It all starts with learning to think differently. Top producers have learned to be aware of what they think, say and do. They have learned their past thoughts and actions produce results that are intimately integrated into the present. Some experiences carry negative influences while other experiences are positive reinforcements. Bottom line is it's about learning to reflect on and evaluate how past experiences impact making conscious choices for the current work-life role and activities. Top Producers actively choose to think and act differently, especially as it pertains to the question, *"Does this activity produce value for my clients?"* And, most importantly, they know what they are willing to do and unwilling to do to achieve success. They have clearly defined their values and beliefs.

Ask Yourself

⇒ Am I willing to change old thoughts, beliefs, behaviors and habits?

⇒ Will my new habits serve me or my clients?

⇒ Do I know *specifically* what I need to do and am I *willing* to change?

⇒ Have I clearly defined my personal and professional values and beliefs?

Coaching Works When You Do

- **Commit to fully engage in the process.** It's your job, career, life and the amount of money you make. Make it important to engage and stay engaged. If you have a team, implement this practice there too. Consistent commitment will increase your faith in yourself and what you do. Faith strengthens all you do.

- **Do what you say you will do.** This is a matter of character. Your clients expect you to do what you say you will do. Make commitments and keep them or make appropriate adjustments. Work-life balance here may be a challenge and you have to evaluate the investment you must make to carry through on all there is before you…then you will always get better at taking care of and serving your clients.

- **Be brutally honest with yourself.** Ditto on the character issue. Your clients expect you to be genuine and authentic with them. Treat yourself the same or better by being honest with yourself, first.

- **Decide to change.** If you are not willing to seriously consider changing certain ways you think and things you do, then don't waste your time or the time of a coach or mentor. Just do it or find something else to do.

- **Use the *Ask Yourself* questions** throughout the book to be the catalyst to think differently. Questions can become a power tool for revealing and releasing your untapped potential.

- **Be courageous.** Allow your *Warrior Spirit* to spring forth.

Ask Yourself

Who do you want to be? Someone who...

⇒ Makes it happen,

⇒ Watches it happen,

⇒ Wonders what happens?

Ask Yourself

⇒ How do your disciplines compare to Top Producers?

Both/And Thinking Makes ZFactor a Virtual Master Mind

A unique aspect of the ZFactor proprietary methodology is the use of an *XY* graph as a coaching tool. The *XY* graph naturally encourages *Both/And* thinking when it is customized or adapted to fit a specific situation.

ZFactor has been specifically designed to help you be more of a *Both/And* thinker. The *XY* graph with an *X* axis and *Y* axis offers a simple way to present two different thoughts, opinions or concepts and intersect those together to create an unlimited number of possibilities. Developing this ability to hold two different concepts or thoughts at the same time opens your thinking to new possibilities and ideas. This gives you a real advantage for thinking about how to better serve your clients. You will find yourself creating new ways to approach your clients and the sales situations they present.

You will learn more about this process in the coming pages. When you can learn to hold two different thoughts in your mind at the same time, you will have more capacity to manage a successful selling process.

Self Coaching Guidelines

Use the *PROACT Self Coaching* process on page 44 to familiarize yourself with the coaching process. It is recommended you reference these guidelines until you develop self-coaching into a solid habit. The more you practice self-coaching and understand the value for making it a habit, the faster you will accelerate your sales. The ZFactor methodology leverages *Both/And* thinking with the *XY* graph to empower the self-coaching process.

Self Coaching Reality Check

Take time to work through the following exercises. These exercises will encourage you to think about how and what you do within the context of the Five Disciplines of Top Producers. Remember your journal!

- **Exercise A: Self Coaching Reality Check - How Do You Compare to the Top Producer's Five Disciplines?** Use the Five Disciplines to compare and rate your daily activities and disciplines to that of a Top Producer.

- **ZFactor Accelerator Tool:** *PROACT Self Coaching* process provides you with a set of guidelines to develop a consistent method for self reflection and to develop meaningful plans to achieve your goals and objectives.

Self Coaching is a positive, ongoing process to identify thinking, feeling and speaking patterns that empower you to do those things that accelerate your success—and make you aware of those things to stop doing that slow you down or stop you from achieving all you desire.

Exercise A - Self Coaching Reality Check

How Do You Compare to the Top Producer's Five Disciplines?

You can accelerate your personal and professional development when you think about how to apply a new idea or concept into your daily routine.

Review the Five Disciplines starting on page 35: How do your best business practices and sales disciplines compare to Top Producers?

1. Reflect on Basic Practices and Disciplines.

2. Keep a To Do list, Stop Do and Who Do list.

3. Invest in Personal and Professional Development.

4. Have a *Make It Happen Attitude*.

5. Be Willing To Do What Works.

Take a moment to inventory and create a list of your daily activities to show what you did and the amount of time spent. Include those less disciplined things that don't make you any money, like surfing the internet to find out about your favorite sports team.

⇒ Show the amount of time you spent doing each activity.

⇒ Choose those things you will continue to do because it grows sales.

⇒ Check off the things you will stop doing. The things that don't make you money.

⇒ Based upon this list, reflect on the things you will do and make the commitment to develop the disciplines and practices that define the Five Disciplines of Top Producers and successful sales professionals.

⇒ Get someone to hold you accountable to your commitments to make these changes.

Things I did today	Time Spent	Keep Doing	Stop Doing	Money Spent

Exercise A - Self Coaching Reality Check

How Do You Compare to the Top Producer's Five Disciplines?

Consider How You Compare to Top Producers

- **A Reality Check:** Be brutally honest with yourself as you compare your disciplines with the Five Disciplines of Top Producers.

  - Based upon your responses on the previous page, what is one thing you plan to change that will begin moving you toward being a Top Producer?

  - What challenges do you expect to have in making this change?

  - What are specific things you need To Do, Stop Doing and delegate to others?

- **Execute:** Do what you say you will do. Expect to get better at everything you do.

  - Use the *ZFactor PROACT Self Coaching* process on page 44 to help you think about how to establish the disciplines required to create change in your business. Record the responses to your PROACT process in your journal. You will continue to use this throughout the ZFactor acceleration process.

  - Take responses from the first part of this exercise and create your final (and first of many) Stop Do and Start Do lists.

Your Notes Here:

ZFactor Accelerator Tool
ZFactor PROACT Self Coaching Process

The guidelines below empower the ZFactor Self Coaching Methodology. This guides you through a thinking process to discover your own answers. Use with a coach or self-reflection. Write your thoughts in your journal.

P **Prepare** Yourself to Turn Thoughts into Actions	• Block out time at least once a week for a self coaching session. The more frequent the sessions the faster the results. • Be consistent. Keep sessions at the same time and location. Keep a journal. • Self-awareness. Desire to have deep understanding and to know yourself and skills. • Ask the hard questions and be brutally honest. Be curious with the desire to learn new things and how to apply new skills, behaviors. • Learn to easily assimilate information and data. Use it or lose it. Action orientation. • Always be willing to accept instructions, advice, critique, counsel and mentoring.
R **Review** Where You Are	• Review since last session. Celebrate accomplishments and focus on key needs. • What has been accomplished since last session? • What actions did you complete or not complete?
O **Objectives** Where Do You Want To Be	• Establish 3 objectives you want to accomplish in the week. • Identify 2 relationships to move forward. • Identify 1 revenue producing initiative or sale to close or move to close. • What do you want to accelerate? What is most important for you to accomplish?
A **Assess** Ask Yourself the Hard Questions	• Use the *Ask Yourself* questions in the book to stimulate your thoughts. • What is next for you? What will you Do - Stop Do - decide Who Do - change or tweak? • What is your biggest challenge now or greatest need? • Who can be a resource for you to help you make changes and what will be your request? • What will you complete before your next session?
C **Create** Establish Action Plan	• **To Do List:** group into priorities Must Get Done (MGD), Should Get Done (SGD), Could Get Done (CGD) • **Stop Do List:** list of activities, behaviors, attitudes you will stop doing because they have a low payoff or no value. • **Who Do List:** list of activities you can delegate to others. Must be easy to train and essential for business growth.
T **Timed** For Success	• Block out times for making money – first – such as closing sales and prospecting for the pipeline development. Fill in marketing, administrative, relationship, sales follow up activities. • Keep doing what makes money and find ways to improve these activities. • What are you committed to? What are you willing to do that will achieve your goals? • When will each of the actions be completed? Given where you are now what will it take for you to get to where you want to be. What is a realistic timeline to complete?

Ask Yourself

Ask Yourself after each coaching session (record in your journal)

⇒ How are you committed to change and reinforcing a strong desire to achieve more?

⇒ How are you prepared to grow, both professionally and personally?

⇒ What more do you desire for yourself, your business and family?

⇒ How are you acting differently to achieving and exceeding goals and objectives?

⇒ What is next as an investment of time/money into developing the business and the work-life you desire?

⇒ How do you plan to release any concerns or fears you have about making changes that will improve who you are and where you are?

⇒ What specifically will you focus on this week to accelerate your sales, achieve top producer status and continue on the road to become a Value Creator?

Do all you can do and then do more. Believe in that moment when everything works and you realize more potential is released than you have ever imagined.

PART TWO

THE ⓩ FACTOR

SALES ACCELERATOR

Part Two Introduction

The ZFactor Sales Accelerator

Congratulations! You have made it to this point and you should have a better sense for the things you need *To Do* and *Stop Doing*. If you truly want to build a successful and sustainable business, you must master the basics, best sales disciplines and business practices. *Product Basics* is the cornerstone of the *Sales Growth ZMap*. When you realize how well executed sales basics improve your sales results, you are ready to learn how to accelerate sales.

Part One focused on why and how to think and act differently. If you change your thinking, you can change your results. Learning to think differently helps you deal with the unknown and manage all the changes you have to make. You can use the *ZFactor Self-Coaching* skills to accelerate any work-life process you choose to improve. When you fully develop these skills, and focus on creating value for clients, that's when you really experience acceleration and better results.

Part Two of the ZFactor methodology solidifies Part One and focuses on how to cross the gap between where you *are now* in your business, and where you *want to be*.

Sales Acceleration Made Simple

Top Producers know *how* to think about *what* they do and then find ways to make what they do, better. They may not even be able to explain how they do this. They just do it. When you speak with a Top Producer their *Warrior Spirit* is clear and present. By the way they speak, you know they have the courage to face the future and the unknowns. They have learned how to leverage their strengths and manage all the changes sales professionals must make to achieve success. But if we try to do something exactly the way they do it—that is a waste of time. That's why how to books and

If what you do isn't making money for you or creating value for your clients, then stop doing it. Do what works and keep doing it until it doesn't work and then find something new that works.

The greatest ROI you will ever experience is when you make thinking a productive skill.

sales recipes can only work with minimal success. It is more valuable for you to *know yourself* and *your strengths*, first, and then learn how to integrate and adapt the best traits of value creators who are most similar with you. In this way you leverage *your* talents, strengths and skills to become more and more effective.

Skillful, disciplined thinking differentiates a Top Producer from an average producer. The title of the book *Think and Grow Rich* by Napoleon Hill stated the obvious. You have to think about something first before you can have it. If you can't imagine it and believe it, you will not have it.

It isn't just about thinking differently. It's about listening to yourself think, managing your thoughts and being aware of the results of your actions. It is a powerful experience when you truly understand how results occur when thoughts are combined with acting differently. If you can't control what you think, you won't know what to do that works. Disciplined thinking has a very high return on the time invested in thinking and planning. Expect there to be struggles and expect to win. Keep at it until you do.

ZFactor simplifies the process for learning how to think differently with the ZMaps. Each ZMap is specifically customized to help you develop a consistent thinking strategy for organizing your plans and actions to produce the results you desire.

Three Types of Sales Professionals

Pat has come to realize his success is really a matter of thinking and acting like a successful professional. A really simple thought Pat turned into a habit has been, *If what you do isn't making you money or creating value for your clients, then stop doing it.*

In very simplistic terms, there are three types of sales professionals:

1. The first one takes on the *Warrior Spirit* and believes they work in a noble profession because they focus on serving the client and doing all that's best to create value for clients. They begin believing, thinking and acting like successful people they desire to model and continually strive to achieve their sales, business, career and work-life objectives. Personal potential is fully realized. Using an

> Without a clear, thoughtful plan and working that plan, thinking differently is like watching a TV reality show and wishing that was you.
>
> Top Producers make their own adventures.

exercise analogy, this is the person who has a fairly consistent diet and exercise routine and has energy and stamina to lead an active lifestyle—essentially being able to do anything they want.

2. The second has the desire to make some changes, but gets bogged down by life and other challenges along the way. This type starts out of the gate at a fast pace each time they initiate to make changes, makes some slight improvements, but tends to fall back into easier habits or allows distractions to get in the way. They tell themselves they are satisfied for the most part or that it just is *what it is*. Yet, a glowing ember of their potential nags at them for them to fully apply themselves as they ponder on when that *one day* will come and they finally make the change. Don't take this wrong, one can still be successful here. Yet, they always have that nagging thought of their untapped potential and *know* this is a constant cycle throughout their life. The analogy here, would be the person who starts the diet or exercise routine, but always seems to back-slide. They do enough to have a foundation of health, but never really achieve the ultimate goal long-term.

3. The third is pretty comfortable with where they are now, and for whatever reasons, they have stuffed away their ambition to achieve more. They know they have potential for much more, but are just not quite willing to do what it takes to realize it. Ironically, just a few minutes a day dedicated to reflection and forward-looking goal setting would set the stage for when the right moment hits with a spark to re-ignite them. Ask yourself—if the perfect business opportunity came along, could you *sprint* to take advantage of it?...Or have you let your *business muscles* atrophy so that the ability to be agile and responsive is out of use? Use them or lose them. Your choice.

> **You really are who you think you are. If you really want things to change, change your thinking and start doing things that work.**

Ask Yourself

⇒ Which type of sales professional are you today?

⇒ What three things could you do to improve and become the sales professional you want to be?

"Thought leads to actions."

~ James Allen ~

James Allen teaches two essential truths:

- *"Today we are where our thoughts have taken us, and*

- *we are the architects, for better or worst, of our futures."*

We want to encourage all three types to proceed into Part Two. Yes, there is more of a time commitment, but you've put yourself on the path to achieving success. Why delay? Perhaps you will see some of yourself as Pat moves on and advances, grows sales and builds his business toward the Fourth Quadrant, *Value Creator*.

Back in the Coffee Shop after Several Weeks

"Pat, you made the comment several weeks ago that you planned to make several changes in how you do business. Give me an example of one thing you changed and how it is making a difference for you."

"This is going to sound silly and it seems like I've heard it hundreds of times. *Do the things that make money and stop doing what doesn't make money.* I finally took that concept to heart after reviewing the *Five Disciplines of Top Producers* and completing the *ZFactor Self-Coaching Reality Check*. Those two things helped me focus on the right things to do to get sales back on track.

"What did you stop doing, Pat?"

"Just a couple of examples of things I stopped doing. I turned off the radio and stopped listening to the talk shows driving to appointments. I now use that time to think, listen to podcasts, or make personal phone calls. I also shut down some of the email feeds I had subscribed to that weren't really business related and gave up my fantasy league play. Most importantly, I started shutting down my email for at least one hour a day and stopped checking every single email when it came in. Now I always turn it off when making calls and during training or informational webinars."

"So, what did you start doing with all that time, Pat?"

"You laugh, but I was amazed at how much time I wasted on stuff like that and entertaining myself. It shocked me to realize how much time I spent on those things and how much that sucked me away from doing what makes money and builds my business. I also realized I would take calls and answer email as a way to not have to do the harder stuff—like make the tough calls. I even lulled myself into believing the time I spent discussing my fantasy teams with other people online was a way to prospect. I've got a buddy that I suspect considers his weekly golf outings in the same way. It's embarrassing to admit this, but it hit me upside the head like a sledge hammer when I realized how lazy I was about my daily work habits and personal disciplines. What's really amazing about this—I would do those things and at the end of the day still wonder why my sales weren't better. Talk about being unconsciously incompetent."

"So, Pat, you have proven to yourself that the concept of change your thinking, change your results is true?"

"You bet. As I've changed my thinking toward doing business during business hours, I've noticed how I've changed the way I feel about things like fantasy football. I suppose for younger folks, they are challenged by the various online social media sites, texting and phone apps that take them off point. If I am really serious about accomplishing my goals, then it's really very simple. Keep my attention and focus strictly on business, during business hours."

"That's interesting, Pat. I do remember when I thought my time playing golf was prospecting. In fact, I had a saying, *"the more golf I play the more money I make."* The truth is the more golf I played the more money it cost. I still enjoy golf, but now I play because I enjoy it. I do consider it a way to further develop my relationships, and see the value in that. But, those results are not directly monetary. I stopped fooling myself. Only, it took me longer to figure it out than for you. I had buddies in the business who wanted to hold on to the old way. When I stopped, they kept trying to get me to come back and they gave me a hard time about not playing as much golf. And, when I did play with them, they really enjoyed giving me a hard time about my scores."

"So, what did you do? Because my buddies are giving me a hard time, as well."

"You just have to move on, Pat. Not to brag, but my total revenues equal several of my buddies' businesses added together. And it's not like my golf score is going to put money in my pocket. If you love to golf, make time for it *after* the work day is done!"

"As a single footstep will not make a path on the earth, so a single thought will not make a pathway in the mind. To make a deep physical path, we walk again and again. To make a deep mental path, we must think over and over the kind of thoughts we wish to dominate our lives."

~ Henry David Thoreau ~

53 Z

A big difference between an average producer and a top producer is the top producer has the will and determination to do what works.

"That's awesome, and nice to hear you are a normal guy, Terry. Since I've stopped listening to talk radio and all, I've started listening to recordings of industry experts. I pause the recordings when I hear a tip or idea that sounds like it would make a difference for me. Then I think about a prospect I'm trying to develop or future meeting I need to plan for a client. I now spend much more time thinking about various scenarios to create more value for clients. I can already sense some changes in how I'm speaking and my confidence has returned because I'm staying focused on my business and my clients."

"Pat, when we first got together, it sounded like you just let yourself drift away from the basics. Now that you have more consistent daily sales practices working for you again, sounds like you are ready start moving along this journey and with the right kind of focus."

"Terry, I am, and I've got lots of questions."

"I understand, Pat. You have put best business practices back into your daily sales activities. That is essential for moving forward into these next parts of ZFactor. Most sales professionals will tell you they want to be a top producer, but few are willing to do what it takes. I can see you are willing to not only do what it takes, I believe you are going to make it happen."

"Thanks, Terry"

Ask Yourself

Are You Ready to Move Forward?

⇒ How would you compare yourself to Pat? Have you stopped doing things that don't make you money?

⇒ Did you replace those things you have stopped doing with activities that will increase sales and build a solid business?

⇒ What changes are you making in your sales and business goals?

⇒ How do you plan to maximize those changes?

⇒ Are you using the PROACT template on a weekly basis to guide the development of you and your business?

Chapter 2.1

Measure Reality... Reveal Potential...

Many want to *be* a top producer. Few will *do* what it takes to have the results of the top producer. The average producer will take a few minutes, guess at some sales targets and call that goal setting. Some even refer to that as planning. Most will spend less than thirty minutes to go through a goal setting or business planning exercise quarterly. They want to achieve the goal, but are never willing to make the necessary changes required to reach their goals. And, they will wonder why they just never achieve their goals.

Top Producers have a different way of thinking about what they do and the results they produce.

Measure Reality... Reveal Potential...

Pat has come a long way in a short period of time. It began with being brutally honest with himself to assess the reality of his situation. While Terry was available as an accountability partner, Pat took responsibility for his situation and did what had to be done to get out of his sales slump. As Pat dug deeper into knowing more about himself and his clients, he began to have a few revelations. By simply putting basic sales disciplines back into his daily activities, the result was a rapid and positive impact on sales results.

An unexpected benefit of working with Terry and ZFactor was that Pat has started to focus more on his clients as opposed to being focused on just making the sale. The more he does the right things with the right people at the right time, the more Pat's confidence grows with each client meeting. He becomes bolder in helping others understand the value of his services and how his expertise is essential to helping his customer stakeholders achieve their long term business objectives. Prospects and clients are responding positively and Pat now has a glimpse into how and why top producers are so different.

Top Producers do as Thoreau described. They think about what they do or want to do over and over until it becomes the dominant thought and begins to drive their results.

Top Producers reflect on the link between *what* they think and *why* they do business the way they do it.

So,,, Why are Top Producers Different?

Top Producers are different mainly because of *how* they think about *what* they do. Think about a few top producers you know. Are they all the same? Do they all think and do everything the same way? Do they all sell to the same clients with the same products? Of course not. This is a key point to consider. Every top producer is different in how they think and what they do. They each have very different backgrounds, skills, strengths, life experiences, knowledge, education, values, behaviors and beliefs—and they know how to *leverage* them. The only key trait shared by all successful people is they spend time thinking about who they are, who their clients are and how to leverage the resources they have (or need) to create value for those around them.

Top Producers invest time and money in personal and professional development because any effort invested in knowing who they are, where they are, and where they want to be, has a very high return on investment. The dividends from this investment solidify a growing belief in themselves and their ability to contribute to the well being of those with whom they choose to engage. Their beliefs develop and deepen with each achievement and they gain a deeper understanding of how the value of their ideas, products and solutions create value for their clients. As they continue to operate their business based upon these values, beliefs and principles, what they do and how they do it becomes immeasurably important. This is why Top Producers are different.

When Pat and Terry first bumped into one another in the North Side Coffee Shop, Terry showed Pat the *Sales Growth ZMap* on page 15. This started Pat thinking very differently about business. Pat now uses ZMap as a new thinking tool and framework to organize and clarify his thoughts and actions toward his goals and objectives—something he now refers to as *Value Creator*. Even though he still has many more questions than answers about the concept of *Value Creator*, he has envisioned something bigger than his frustrations over day-to-day sales results.

The next chapter shows how Pat begins gaining new clarity about where he is and who and where he wants to be. This chapter converts the *Sales*

Growth ZMap from just a static map to more like a GPS (Global Positioning System or as we like to call it, *Goal Positioning System* for your business.

Think of the Growth of your Business as a Journey

Become the person you want to be and achieve your goals. Become a *Value Creator*. Consider these four steps as you continue this journey.

1. **Know Who You Are.** Know your strengths and weaknesses as they compare to top producers' characteristics. Decide to get better at everything you do. Take time for self coaching, join an accountability group or engage a professional business coach to help you plan your work and work your plan.

2. **Know Where You Are and Where You Want to Be.** Use the Sales Growth ZMap. Keep a journal of your progress, complete the exercises in the book and use the tools on a regular basis to construct a living, dynamic action plan.

3. **Plan Your Journey.** Know what you have to do, who you have to know, and what resources are necessary to get you to where you want to be.

4. **Continue to Learn and Develop Yourself.** Complete the *ZFactor Self-Assessment*, find other self assessments and read other books to help you learn more about yourself.

> You know you are committed when you get someone else to hold you accountable to do what you say you will do.

Ask Yourself

⇒ Are you clear about where you are in your sales performance and business development? If not, what do you need to become clear?

⇒ Is there something you have wanted to change, but you just haven't done it yet? Do you know what's holding you back? How will it create value for you and your clients? Is there someone you can get to hold you accountable?

⇒ How would you rate your goal setting process? What will it take to get even more serious about goal setting and achieving your goals?

Chapter 2.2

ZFactor Self-Assessment
New Business Growth Starts Here

"The unexamined life is not worth living."

~ Socrates ~

The ZFactor Self-Assessment is a simple assessment that quickly provides a **Your Are Here** marker on the ZMap. You have to know *where you are* to chart the course for *where you want to go*. You will review four statements to help you assess performance and development improvements you can make in order to accelerate your sales. Studies show when an individual honestly engages in a self assessment, they are more willing to set realistic goals and commit to making changes. Self assessing who you are, your strengths and weaknesses, attitudes, desires and behaviors, habits and values, is essential for making substantial improvement in sales performance.

The ZFactor Self-Assessment has been customized to be a simple and quick guide for sales professionals selling products. The goal is to provide specific input so you can begin to move from being a *vendor* who competes on price to a *value creator* for whom there are no rivals.

...move from being a vendor who competes on price to a value creator for whom there are no rivals.

You will be encouraged to focus your thoughts and actions on specific practices, characteristics, disciplines and behaviors of success. Take time to do some self-reflection and self coaching as this will encourage you to become more disciplined in your thoughts and actions. Remember to use the *PROACT Self Coaching* process on page 44.

Of course this will take some time and we fully believe you will experience an exponential return on investment for any amount of time invested in an organized, focused self reflection process with ZFactor.

Three steps to take before you begin your journey.

1. Know where you are.

2. Know who you are.

3. Plan your journey.

The Purpose of the ZMap Self-Assessment

- The ZMap Self-Assessment encourages you to consider your strengths and weaknesses as it relates to defining characteristics of successful sales professionals.

Resistance to new thinking is futile and will cost you money.

- This self assessment is not a scientific diagnostic tool. It is designed to help you compare thoughts about your sales disciplines and business practices relative to those disciplines and practices clearly understood and proven by successful professionals as essential for building a successful, sustainable and significant business.

- Every journey has a starting place and a destination. The ZMap Self-Assessment will give you a *Starting Quadrant,* and your destination or *Target Quadrant* becomes the next quadrant along the backward Z. For example, if you assess yourself to be in the second quadrant (Preferred Status), your *Target Quadrant* would be the third quadrant (Program Mastery).

- In this chapter, the *Sales Growth ZMap* now shows labels for the *X* and *Y* axes. *X* axis—*Hard to Replace. Y* axis—*Strategically Important.*

Ask Yourself

⇒ **How do you become *Strategically Important and Hard to Replace* with your clients?**

The value in thinking about this question as you take the assessment is that it stimulates you to have a new and very different mindset about how you perceive yourself and your clients. Notice how this sentence above carries two distinct objectives to be considered at the same time – making this another of the *Both/And* questions discussed earlier. There are many other sales professionals selling similar products to your prospects and clients. What will make you distinctive above your competition and have your clients value you, your services, and your expertise? What makes you *strategically important* and *hard to replace*?

Considering this question empowers the *ZFactor Self-Assessment* and helps you laser in on where you are relative to becoming a *Value Creator* for your clients.

Summary of the Following Pages

- **Review—Preparation and Reflection** helps you develop a new mindset for completing the self-assessment.

- **ZFactor Self-Assessment** is the assessment on page 64.

- **Identify your Starting and Target Quadrants:** This foundational information and your starting and target quadrants on page 65 will be used throughout the rest of the book.

People who honestly engage in a self assessment are more willing to make changes that work.

Preparation and Reflection
for ZMap Self-Assessment

Ask Yourself: How do you become *Strategically Important* and *Hard to Replace* with your clients?

Strategically Important and *Hard to Replace* are the axes labels on this ZMap. This single question can very quickly bring forth very different thoughts from different professionals. It is very effective at creating a new mindset. These axes labels add much more depth to the *Value Creator* concept. How to become *Strategically Important* and *Hard to Replace* should be the primary question for any aspiring *Value Creator*. This question should cause you to pause and ponder throughout the time you utilize ZFactor. The question will alter how you think and the actions you take, which in turn will dramatically accelerate you and your business to bigger results for you and your clients.

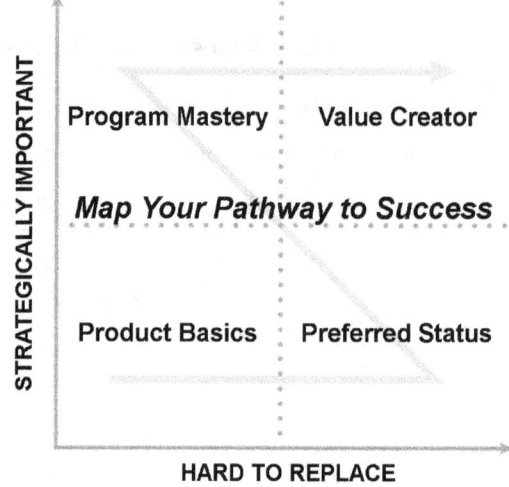

Here are a few examples of when you know you are being *Strategically Important* and *Hard to Replace* with your clients.

Hard to Replace	Strategically Important
• You know what is important to your clients and what really matters to them. They depend on you.	• You know your products and resources and how to leverage these to create new solutions.
• Your clients know you are deeply interested in them and their special interests. They know you value them.	• You easily create innovative solutions customized to each client's unique needs. You pull things together for the client.
• You provide a distinctive high quality service above all other standards. You don't think about competition. You are the competition.	• You build sustainable solutions and your clients recognize you for that.
• You have a clear communications plan with each client. They know how to reach you and vice versa.	• You know how and when to leverage right people, resources, best practices at the right time.
• Your clients know the significant value you have created for them and refer others to you.	• You consistently deliver high value.
	• You think and do things differently and at a higher quality than your competition.

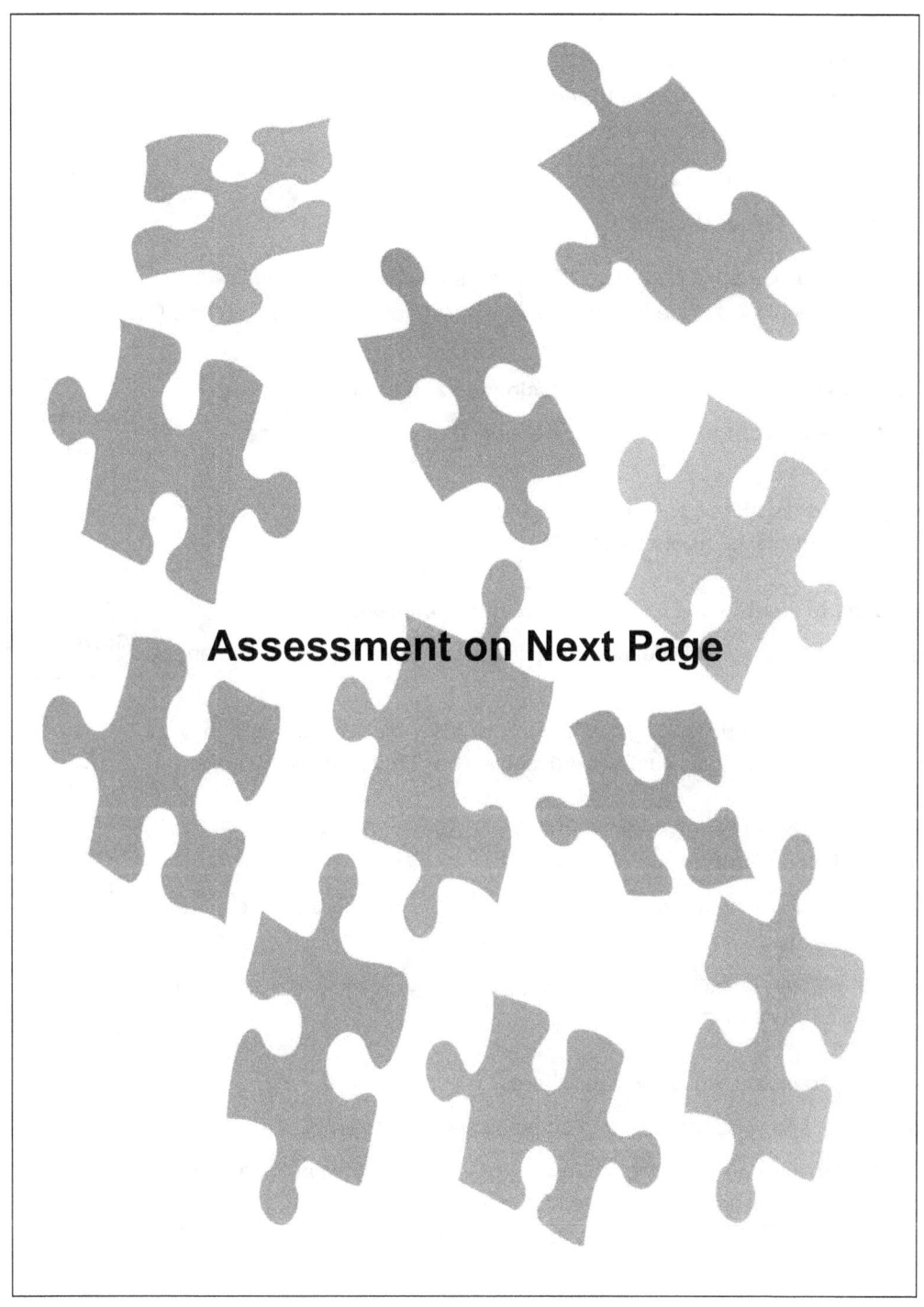

Assessment on Next Page

ZMap Self-Assessment

Map Your Pathway to Success with ZMap

How *Strategically Important* and *Hard to Replace* are you with your clients? Keep this question in mind as you rank yourself based upon the four statements below. Every journey has two primary components:

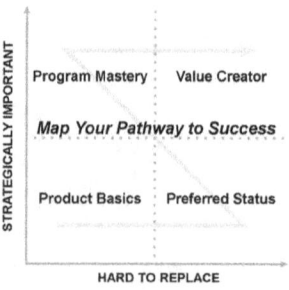

1. Starting point or **Starting Quadrant**.
2. Destination or **Target Quadrant**.

To assess your *Starting Quadrant*, read each of the four statements below and rate your answers 1 to 6. Then, look to the facing page 65 to get your *Starting and Target Quadrant*.

1. Rate the consistency of your daily sales disciplines and business practices.

⇒ 1 is "My sales disciplines, time management and practices tend to be inconsistent."

⇒ 6 is "My sales disciplines and practices have remained consistent for a year or more and my sales results prove it."

Score for # 1	

2. Rate your ability to identify and be referred to your ideal client.

⇒ 1 is "I do not have a clearly defined ideal client. I still take any client and any referral."

⇒ 6 is "I am providing outstanding services for my ideal clients and they consistently refer me to highly qualified prospects who fit my ideal client profile."

Score for # 2	

3. Rate your ability to be a trusted vendor and provide your clients relevant, unparalleled results.

⇒ 1 is "I focus on making the sale rather than engaging in understanding more about my client's business."

⇒ 6 is "I consistently deliver solid business solutions that produce relevant and measurable results for my clients."

Score for # 3	

4. Rate your ability to create value for your clients.

⇒ 1 is "I do not fully understand how to create value for my clients."

⇒ 6 is "My clients and professional network express their appreciation for my expertise and the value I have created for them. I am strategically important and hard to replace with repeatable, predictable business from my clients."

Score for # 4	

Review your score on the next page for your *Starting Quadrant*.

My Total Score	

Identify Your Starting and Target Quadrants

Know Where You Are

1. Review the **ZMap Quadrant Quick Definitions** on the right side of page.

2. Match your **Total Score** to the scores in the **ZMap Scoring Chart.**

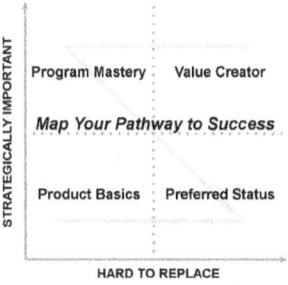

ZMap Scoring Chart

Match your Score to Scores Below	ZMap Quadrant [Quadrant Definitions in sidebar]
4 - 7	Product Basics
8 -11	Preferred Status
12 - 19	Program Mastery
20 - 24	Partner and Value Creator

3. Write the name of your **Starting ZMap Quadrant.**

My Starting Quadrant	

4. Write the name of your **Target ZMap Quadrant.**

My Target Quadrant	

5. **Read the Quadrant Definitions in the sidebar:** Read the definitions for your *Starting and Target Quadrant.*

Ask Yourself

⇒ What in your *Starting Quadrant* definition confirms you being in that quadrant?

⇒ What strengths do you have that can be leveraged to move you toward your *Target Quadrant*?

⇒ What new strengths do you need to develop or outsource?

ZMap Quadrant Definitions

Do a quick review of the four ZMap quadrant definitions below. Which one clearly relates to you and your current situation?

Product Basics (1)

You have clearly defined daily disciplines and practices that drive your sales basics.

Preferred Status (2)

You consistently receive qualified referrals and personal introductions from your best clients that fit your ideal client profile.

Program Mastery (3)

You have mastered delivery of strategic solutions that exemplify your expertise, knowledge, and skills to create value for your clients.

Partner and Value Creator (4)

You have achieved sustainable business success because your expertise, knowledge and skills have made a significant difference for your clients.

Ask Yourself

⇒ Who are your top five clients now?

⇒ What product or solution works best for them?

Terry Reviews Pat's Self-Assessment

"Pat, what did you think about the self-assessment?"

"It's really simple. I was expecting it to be a lot more involved, but it's less like an assessment and more like a thinking tool. It made me pause and consider *IF* I am being strategically important and hard to replace with my clients. If so, then how am I doing that. *AND*, if I'm not, what do I need to be doing. You can see by my score I've got a long way to get to *Value Creator*."

Pat's Total Score	**10**
Pat's Starting Quadrant	**Preferred Status**
Pat's Target Quadrant	**Program Mastery**

"Pat, I know you will become a Value Creator. It's clear you have put yourself back on the right track by dedicating time to embrace the basic sales disciplines and practices. How did you score yourself on the first statement?"

"I gave myself a five because of how consistent my daily activities are now and I understand why the basics are so important for my sustainable success. I'm not a six because I've only been consistent with my new work habits for a couple of months."

"Good. So, how did you rate yourself on identifying and being referred to your ideal client?"

"This one made me think about how I am asking for and getting referrals. What I realized—if the client values your service—and believes you are *hard to replace*, they are more likely to have you top of mind when others with their company or network need similar products and services. Bottom line is I don't have a consistent approach for being that *preferred resource*, and I don't have a true discipline for requesting referrals. Remember the day we reconnected in the coffee shop and I had the prospect cancel on me? She has turned out to be a great client, and I see lots of growth and opportunity there. I was referred to her, but that was more luck than clearly knowing who my ideal client is. Then, my Dad referred me to a friend of his who had just been promoted to a key procurement position. I realized I didn't have the expertise to understand how to create value for him. He expected a good price on products as a given and wanted to know how my services would be different. I guess you could say he wanted to know why the next guy, like me, wouldn't just lower the price and take my place. What an embarrassing meeting that was. I wasn't even close to being prepared. So, I gave myself a three for that statement. I need to define my ideal client and understand why they would prefer to do business with me beyond price. Then I need to determine what is the key role I want to sell to within the client, based on where I am today. I've been so focused on pursuing any and all sales opportunities, I've not taken the time to really explore the characteristics of my ideal client and why they would prefer doing business with me. I figured you could help me out with this."

"Yes, I can, Pat. It's not a complicated process, but takes some time for reflection and review. You start by looking at where you have been or believe you could be successful—*specifically*. This means looking at your current strong relationships, clients and their key relationships, their roles, their industries and identifying the best scenarios where you can create reoccurring revenue. Usually this is where the client has a budget or at least a plan in place for why and when they buy—including *why* it is from you—if you have that knowledge. You may or may not have an ideal or highly successful situation in place yet, but you start with where you believe the opportunities might be. You really want to focus on long-term clients who can provide what is called *life time value*—meaning a relationship beyond just one sale. Then you begin researching and networking to do two things: first, look within your existing clients to find other potential relationships that you could be referred; and, second, use your network to identify potential prospects that have a similar profile.

Often times, a new sales professional hears that a specific industry or even job title is the perfect target market, but they don't have connections, education or experience to help them develop a plan. The best way to determine your current ideal client profile is to identify a set of your top clients now. What were the products or solutions they purchased? How have you become hard to replace? Why do they prefer doing business with you?

Completing a client profile takes little time and has a very high return on investment.

Clearly identify specific characteristics of these clients. Write these down and reflect on them and then let your clients know you are looking for people who have a similar situation. Look into your network and see who you know, and who will introduce you to others or to an organization that has needs similar to your ideal client profile. Just as you are progressing along the ZMap, your ideal client profile will change as you grow and develop in the business.

"Another fascinating aspect of the methodology is that you can also plot your *clients*—and as you grow in skill, so will the type of client you attract. For example, does the prospect only expect bids, or do they also want a level of service they are not getting from someone else, at this time? Remember it takes time to develop as a preferred provider and cultivate a truly consistent referral program. The key is to stick with it and refine all areas as you grow and develop yourself and your business."

"Sounds like I just need to take some time to reflect on my existing client base and to identify my ideal client scenario. So I guess, I hope, that I also focus on where I have the most fun or feel the most competent—like with a certain title or position or with a certain type of sale?"

"You got it, Pat. It is all about getting started on this process. It doesn't matter *where* you are now, it matters where you are going. As you build your client base using your ideal client profile, it will become much easier to move into other types of ideal clients. We can talk more about that later. But, let's finish up on how you scored your assessment."

"Well, the last couple of statements were pretty easy to score. I have not spent a lot of time understanding my clients' business, let alone how they could measure results from working with me. Also, I can honestly say I don't understand who I have to be or what I must do to be considered a Partner and *Value Creator*. I have ideas, but nothing that rates me above a one for each of the last two statements."

"Good to see you being honest with yourself. We will discuss more about becoming a partner and value creator later. That's what I like about how the Defining Characteristics have been segmented to each quadrant. It helps you focus on what you need today and helps you plan for future development. By reviewing the characteristics in all the quadrants, you may not be

"The purpose of life is not to be happy. It is to be useful, to be honorable, to be compassionate, to have it make some difference that you have lived and lived well"

~ Ralph Waldo Emerson ~

Z 68

able to rate yourself very high in every area, but you can shift your thinking and start practicing, today. In fact, the process of identifying your ideal client will help you hear the prospect's comments differently and you will respond to them differently—because you now know you are on this path."

"Man, I hadn't thought about hearing their comments differently. Such as, are they responding to what I sell as a commodity or are they trying to see how I might replace a current solution they have in place? Obviously if I can make myself a preferred resource, it just seems natural my opportunities will get bigger. I'm excited about what I can do and say differently in my next meeting. I'm excited about the possibility of being viewed as more than just another vendor."

"Good for you Pat. So, that means your *Starting Quadrant* now is *Preferred Status* and your *Target Quadrant* is *Program Mastery*. Let's take a look at a new ZMap called the *Sales Accelerator ZMap*. This ZMap lays out the basic *ZFactor Sales Accelerator* methodology. This will help you to dive deeper into your *Starting Quadrant* so you can learn what it takes to master that quadrant and provide you with what you need to know to move yourself toward your *Target Quadrant*. Let's do a quick overview.

"Follow the backward *Z* on the *Sales Accelerator ZMap*. The *X* axis is *Think Differently* and the *Y* axis is *Act Differently*. It takes thinking differently about who and where you are now and who and where you want to be to build a solid foundation for becoming a *Partner and Value Creator*. As you empower your *Warrior Spirit* to act differently, you *embrace the Defining Characteristics of success.* As you put all this together you will find yourself doing what *Value Creators* do."

"Terry, I'm enjoying expanding my thinking to include the *Both/And* thinking strategy and these new axes titles on the ZMap are interesting. Now I see much of all this is simply discipline applied with common sense, but I have not reflected on my business and what I have to do to be successful in such a simple way. I get why it is so important to first focus on thinking and acting differently—and why it is critical to make myself strategically important and hard to replace. As I change my thoughts and actions and embrace the defining characteristics of top producers, I see how I can continually use this to think through how to build a sustainable, successful business."

Before ZFactor Pat didn't put much thought into how to grow a successful business.

Sales Accelerator ZMap

See full size ZMap on page 73.

Some have referred to ZMap as a one page book. It provides a simple, common sense concept with a way to think about how to organize your knowledge, skills and expertise to achieve success.

"You got it, Pat. The next couple of chapters will give you a few tools to help put this all together for building that successful business."

"I'm truly amazed at how dense I've been about focusing on doing what will make me successful. I've just been charging out there to sell, sell, sell without a thought, thought, thought! I feel like I've been stumbling around in the dark. It's as if this has turned the lights on for me."

"Pat, what you feel is very normal. Every top producer experiences this same sense of revelation when they make *THE* decision that changes everything for them and puts them on the pathway to success. The closest other analogy I have for this is running a marathon. When someone decides to run a marathon they don't get out of bed and run 26 miles that day! They have to know where they are, what their current status and pace is and then build a plan to take them from their current ability toward their goal. It's a holistic view that includes stamina, strength and even nutrition. One could say something similar about the game of chess. A true master knows his moves several plays ahead. Think about it. What if you put that effort into your business—or just a fraction of that effort? ZFactor helps you consider all the elements required to produce success over a period of time. Now you have a simple map to guide you into new sets of realizations all along the way, especially when you fully engage yourself into these processes."

It Really is Simple

How about for you, the reader? Any lights coming on for you or new revelations about yourself and how you approach your business? Are you realizing just how simple it can be to focus on specific tactics to increase your sales and achieve higher levels of success? Now that you know what to do, it boils down to your willingness to take the necessary actions to achieve success.

Before ZFactor, Pat just did business the way he felt like doing business and never put much thought into how to grow a successful business. He just worked at making new sales each day. It was as if he woke up every morning and was out of a job until he made a sale that day. Pat is moving from this survival mentality toward a sustainable success mindset. Now Pat sets clearly defined goals and reviews his activities and progress toward becoming a *Partner and Value Creator*.

Know Who and Where You Are and Who and Where You Want to Be

These next few chapters will help you put together a simple plan of action to close or cross the *Success Gaps* you have identified for yourself. You now have the basics for building and strengthening the right habits, disciplines and behaviors of top producers to accelerate your sales.

1. Review the *Sales Accelerator ZMap* on page 15 and the quadrant descriptions on page 16.

2. Work through the *PROACT Self Coaching* process on page 44.

3. Review the *Ask Yourself* questions on page 45. Answer the ones relevant to you and record your answers in your journal.

This will help you develop a deeper understanding about who you are and where you want to be and will lay down the foundation for the next two chapters.

"Enthusiasm is one of the most powerful engines of success. When you do a thing, do it with all your might. Put your whole soul into it. Stamp it with your own personality. Be active, be energetic, be enthusiastic and faithful, and you will accomplish your object. Nothing great was ever achieved without enthusiasm."

~ Ralph Waldo Emerson ~

Goals for Engaging in the use of the ZFactor Sales Accelerator

Just follow the *ZMap*. It sounds simple and it is simple. Yet, the average producer will spend more time planning a vacation than they do planning how to achieve their goals. When you follow the *ZMap*, each of the quadrants build upon one another and work together to accelerate success.

- **Assess and Know Who and Where You Are:** You have to know where you are. To know *where you are* means you have to know your strengths, weaknesses and current resources. What are your beliefs, values and principles - who are you at work, home and community? This is like initially programming a GPS unit with your preferences, so you get the information you want. With this you have a starting place and you can measure progress in thinking and acting differently.

- **Explore Who and Where You Want to Be and Identify Your Success Gap:** Once you know where you are and where you want to be, you can easily define and close the gap between the two. Everyone is unique and starts off from a different place. What works for others may not work for you. You have to be willing to explore new possibilities and alternatives and be teachable and coachable. This process will naturally create different thinking, but you have to put it into action to see what fits you. Do what works and stop doing what doesn't work. You can use the Self-Coaching process and some exercises in the next two chapters to put together an action plan.

- **Embrace Defining Characteristics of Success and Cross Your Success Gap:** Read and emulate the Defining Characteristics of successful people. Do what works and learn from their mistakes. From the *Product Basics* through to full competency as a *Partner and Value Creator* with your clients, the difference between the top producer and the average producer will always be in the application of core competencies. Defining Characteristics are evidenced in their work and the skill at which they can adapt and respond to changing needs. It is that clarity at pinnacle moments where thoughts and possibilities manifest as new and successful breakthroughs of action.

- **Being a Partner and Value Creator and Putting it All Together:** "Commit to get better at everything you do." This is where it all comes together. When you have consistently applied yourself in all the other quadrants you will experience a momentum that sustains your business. With a sustainable business you will experience the significance of becoming a Value Creator.

Empower Your Engagement into ZFactor Sales Accelerator with the PROACT Self Coaching Process

⇒ The *PROACT Self Coaching* process on page 44 is an effective guide for helping you think through application of the concepts in ZFactor for your professional development.

This is the *Sales Accelerator ZMap* with the axes titles of *Act Differently* and *Think Differently*. As you focus your thoughts and actions on the defining characteristics of success you will improve your skills and competencies. The better you know yourself and where you want to be, you will achieve all your goals and objectives.

Ask Yourself

⇒ What specific changes will you make to achieve the *Value Creator* quadrant?

⇒ Track your progress here and in your journal.

Sales Accelerator ZMap

Self-Coaching Session

Putting PROACT to Work for You

You are encouraged to use the information from your ZFactor Self-Assessment and this PROACT process to gain deeper understanding about yourself, your business and your clients. This will help you determine what you need to do to achieve your objectives, crystallize goals, develop simple action plans, determine what to stop doing and what to do that makes you money. You can use this process to measure your progress toward your goals. **Date and record your observations and responses in your journal.**

Prepare Yourself to Turn Thoughts into Actions	• Who are you? What are your strengths and weaknesses? What disciplines and characteristics make you successful? • Where are you? Every journey has a starting place. You have to know where you are to know which direction to go to get to where you want to be. • Generally describe the situation you want to change. • What changes need to be made?
Review Where You Are	• How have you been thinking about your situation? What can you improve? • How does your thinking need to change? • What actions have you taken and what actions do you plan to take? • What actions are working for you?
Objectives Where Do You Want To Be	• What is your overall objective? • What is most important for you to accomplish? • What are your 30 day, 90 day and 6 month goals?
Ask Yourself Questions to Review for Each Session	• What will you Do - Stop Do - decide *"Who Do"* - change or tweak? • What is your biggest challenge now? • Who can be a resource for you to help you make changes and what will be your request? • What is the most important thing that must get done?
Create Action Plan	• **To Do List:** group into priorities Must Get Done (MGD), Should Get Done (SGD), Could Get Done (CGD) • **Stop Do List:** list of activities, behaviors, attitudes you will stop doing because they have a low payoff or no value. • **"Who Do" List:** list of the low return of revenue activities for time invested and consideration of who could potentially do those activities instead.
Timed For Success	• Take time to reflect on where you are now and what will it take to get to where you want to be. • Set a weekly plan and specific times for doing what makes money and find ways to improve these activities. • What's next? • What are you committed to?

Ask Yourself

Who are you?

⇒ What primary weakness is most likely to hold you back from achieving your goals? If you don't have an answer for this one, ask someone who really knows you, like a spouse or friend. Be open and available to hear whatever is said.

⇒ What is most important to you? What motivates you? What are you most passionate about?

⇒ What is a concern or fear you have that keeps you from taking the right actions to achieve your goals?

⇒ What do you think is holding you back and preventing you from achieving your full potential? (examples might be behaviors, disciplines, lack of understanding more about other people's behaviors, location, time, your mindset).

Who do you want to be?

⇒ What do you really want to accomplish in business and life?

⇒ Who are you going to help or serve?

⇒ What do you really enjoy doing? Are you doing that, now? If not, when will you start doing it?

⇒ What do you want to be known for?

⇒ How is your Warrior Spirit at work in all this?

Where do you want to be?

⇒ Describe what your business looks like in six months, one year and three years.

⇒ How will others think about you when you achieve your goals?

⇒ What is most important to you about who you want to become? What motivates you? What are you most passionate about?

⇒ What is one thing you have to do to achieve your goals?

⇒ What is a new skill you plan to develop and how will that increase value for your clients?

⇒ What is one thing you have to stop doing to achieve your goals?

⇒ What consumes time and money that doesn't make you money?

There is always another way. Be curious and explore until you find it.

Achieving your full potential requires that you have used life's experiences to strengthen your character.

Chapter 2.3

The ZFactor Sales Accelerator

The Power Take-Off Tool

Strong convictions empower confidence. Top Producers know any and all investment of time and money to improve their skills will have a significant return on revenue (ROR), as it relates to growing their business.

Pat Considers the Bigger Picture

"Pat, what have you learned about yourself working through the last chapter?"

"The biggest realization is that I control how quickly my sales accelerate, or not. No matter what happens with the economy or otherwise, I can choose to hit the accelerator or ignore all we have discussed and make excuses for my current situation. I've learned a lot about myself and how I've kept my foot on the brake, because I either lacked confidence and didn't know what to do or was unwilling to make the changes I needed to make. I won't say I have been lazy, but I certainly haven't pushed myself at all. I know I have been doing things that kept me busy—but a lot of that didn't make me money or develop me to be a better professional. Surprisingly enough, I can't believe just how much I have been attached to the busy work. I realized that if I wasn't working on an order—or there was nothing to do—I almost went into a panic. Now I am focusing on replacing those old reactive habits with proactive tasks based on a plan. It is so clear to me just how easy it is to go reactive, actually even a little ballistic at times. I can't believe I used to think I didn't need a set weekly plan to be successful. I'm amazed I've been able to attain any of my personal goals. Now, with a plan, I'm ready to really challenge myself."

"Pat, I like your analogy of hitting the brake or the accelerator. That reminds me of the time I got to drive a drag car on a drag racing strip in Houston. Talk about having to think differently. Going from zero to hitting 140

> You have a choice to put your foot on the brake or on the accelerator.

Skill Development ZMap

Accomplishment ZMap

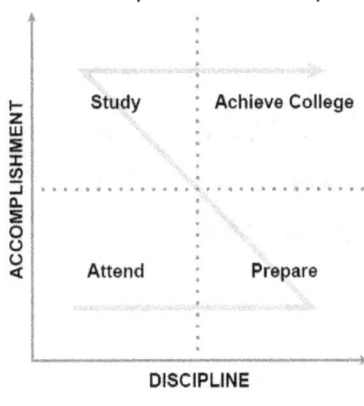

miles per hour in less than ten seconds is very different from driving on the on-ramp up to 70 mph. The first couple of times I raced, I just crammed down on the accelerator and held on to the steering wheel. It seemed like the race was over and my brain was still at the starting line. After a few runs I learned how to speed up my thinking so I was fully aware throughout the entire race—all nine or ten seconds of it that is!"

"So, what you are saying is, we can't just put the pedal to the metal and expect sales productivity to take a quantum leap just because if looks like we're going fast."

"You got it. This next phase of ZFactor covers how to focus on specific sales skills and business practices relative to your ideal target profile for clients. This is designed to help you become aware of the things that produce greater value for clients. Let's take a look at this next ZMap. As you work though the *Skill Development ZMap* consider the right skills and behaviors required to create value for your clients."

"Terry, this is the third ZMap we've worked with and each is different. How many ZMaps are there?"

"That's what makes ZFactor interesting. The methodology is always the same, and is based on an *XY* graph with axes that can be customized to fit a myriad of situations. I've found that ZMaps can help different people quickly shift an unproductive mindset to a more productive mindset. You can literally label the *X* and *Y* axes with any two concepts to drive *Both/And* thinking related to any topic. A simple *XY* graph designed with the ZFactor methodology can help people understand how and why it is beneficial for them to shift an old mindset to a new mindset.

"In fact, I've been talking about ZFactor so much with my wife, she sat down with our teenage son to help him think about what he wants to accomplish during high school—or rather to get him focused on getting his head into the game. She kept it really simple and put *Accomplishment* on the *Y* axis and *Discipline* on the *X* axis (see Accomplishment ZMap in sidebar). She explained to Tommy if he wanted to do what it takes to get his class rank up in preparation for college, he had to develop certain study habits and disciplines to accomplish milestones toward the college goal. Each movement along the *Discipline* axis would have a corresponding result as an accomplishment. She put college in the upper right hand quadrant and explained he needed the right disciplines and a focus on the right activities to accomplish his dream of going to the college of his choice. With each acquired discipline the accomplishments would increase. He understood the concept, and they started simply by focusing on the basics—like preparing his homework on time and getting more involved at school."

"So, there must be hundreds of different uses for the ZMap."

"There are and several examples are in the back of the book. They can be referred to as one page books because the whole picture or concept can be summarized on a single sheet of paper. In fact, that makes me think of the book, *The Art of War* and the quote by General Sun Tzu: "*The general who wins many battles makes many calculations in his temple before the battle is fought.*" You see, I use the ZMaps in a lot of different ways. For example, it's an easy way to think about and prepare for meetings and presentations. Who am I meeting with? What do they care about? I have even used it to plot where a *client* is in their *perception* of me and my team. Then I used that to guide discussion on how we can move the relationship to where I want it to be. I find I can quickly think through many different strategies and alternatives, sometimes using the same foundational *XY* axes—Strategically Important / Hard to Replace—and other times I'll play around with other titles to see what it brings up. Again, always *Both/And* thinking…but let's not get ahead of ourselves here."

"Well, Terry, I'm not tracking with you fully yet, but this helps me understand a little more about how you and how other top producer's think. I am, however, beginning to see how important it is to develop a more productive thinking strategy for serving my clients. And, how important it is to have a well thought out plan in place before every meeting."

"Indeed. You can use the next exercise, the *Power Take-Off Tool* to strengthen the way you think about specific situations, people, yourself and skills you need to increase value for your clients."

"What do you mean by power take off tool?"

"So back to that quote from General Sun Tzu about making many calculations in his temple before the actual battle. Change the word 'battle' to

> *"The general who wins many battles makes many calculations in his temple before the battle is fought."*
>
> ~ General Sun Tzu ~

A *Value Creator* has a network of other people who are also *Value Creators*. Make it a habit to refer your clients to the best.

selling situation. The more clearly defined and organized my thinking strategy before a meeting the sharper my focus on key points as I consider multiple possibilities about a specific client and situation. This way I can focus on organizing sales activities and resources around a client's needs so I can make multiple calculations to discover their requirements quickly and accurately. But the most important thing **ZMap Thinking** provides is stimulus for a continuous stream of questions that I can ask before, during and after the meeting!"

"Hmmm...Terry...this is helping me understand a distinction between this and other methods for improving sales. ZFactor describes how to think about developing sales strategies instead of just trying to get me to adopt some new sales tip, tool, asking questions methodology or *how to* technique that works for someone else."

"Exactly, Pat. The next couple of exercises will help you sharpen your focus even further on each unique client to reveal the right approach for them. The exercises are designed to cause you to consider several scenarios before a meeting. How do you think about a client's situation before a meeting, now?"

"Typically, I quickly glance at any notes I've taken or research done on that client. Sometimes I go into LinkedIn or Google+ to see what I can find on the client and/or company. But to be honest, I don't have any sort of consistent thinking or preparation strategy."

"That's pretty normal for the average producer. When you complete these next exercises you will have some insight into what is missing from the skills and knowledge you need to understand where the client or prospect is coming from so you can create value for them. Then, it's up to you to develop those top producer sales skills for yourself. The good news is you will develop your skills to fit you and your situation. That means it will feel natural and you will find yourself being more authentic with your clients."

"I think I understand what you are saying. Remember I told you about my father referring me to a friend of his who had just been promoted in procurement? Well, I had only been in the business for a few months and I came in all ready to share my creative ideas and all the products I could get for him—had my pitch about great prices, yada, yada, yada. I totally neglected to ask questions.

When he asked questions, I was not prepared. So trying to establish a follow-up plan when the meeting was obviously over was pretty awkward. He was nice about it and asked me to get back with him in the Fall. I left not really knowing what was important to him. But, maybe instead of thinking about how embarrassing that was, I can use the questions he asked me to find support from the right person to figure out what he finds valuable in his vendor relationships. Let me ask you this. Even though I still don't know what I need to know to take care of him, could I create value for him by setting up a meeting for you and me to meet with him?"

"Sure, I'd be happy to do that. The best way to learn is to dive into the process. Why don't you tell me a few of the questions he asked you and then let's work through the *Power Take-Off Tool* exercise together."

Terry points to the page titled *ZFactor Power Take-Off Tool* on page 83. "This tool helps you clarify specific skills and knowledge you need to develop or, in this case, collaborate on in order to accomplish a specific objective for a prospect. What are your objectives for meeting with this guy?"

"With your assistance, I can approach Mr. Smith now, rather than waiting until I know everything I need to know. I've got two objectives. Find out where there is potential to work with Mr. Smith and make this a learning experience for me. All I have to do is set up the meeting."

"Okay. Now, let's do what makes us money and create value for Mr. Smith. Let's work through the exercise so you are well prepared when you call to set up a meeting. Remember, it's your relationship that will give you a second chance. Yet, he's going to have a good sense of what's in it for him to make the time for you again."

Pat and Terry Work Through the ZFactor Power Take-Off Tool

Pat has a twofold objective. He wants to find out what the opportunity is for creating new value for Mr. Smith, who was referred by his Father. He is eager to learn more about creating value along with learning what skills he

> Build a network of Value Creators. Your clients will value you and your services even more.

The right knowledge and skills drive better outcomes for clients and accelerate sales results.

needs to develop. Pat wants to develop his own *Power Take-Off Tool*, like Terry has done. Terry uses this time to go through the exercise with Pat to learn as much as he can about Mr. Smith, so they both are well prepared for the initial meeting.

The objective for the Power Take-Off Tool is pretty simple.

- You set an objective or goal. For example, Pat wants to learn the skills for working with procurement professionals within clients.

- You answer the questions for *Learn, Think, Act* and *Accelerate* as it relates to the specific skills you need and the value those skills will be for you and your clients.

The higher the skill and the higher the value, the faster sales accelerate.

1. **Learn** what you need to know to acquire the right skills to create value for your clients.

2. **Think** about specific actions by focusing on what will be effective for working with ideal clients. When you have spent time thinking through your client's situation then plan out and write down your approach for presenting what will create value for them.

3. **Act** on the actions you intend to take for incorporating the skills necessary to be successful into daily disciplines.

4. **Accelerate** your initiatives by incorporating *Both/And* thinking into your daily disciplines. By considering high skills and high value together you accelerate toward your goals and assist your clients to accelerate toward their goals.

Self Coaching—Session 2
ZFactor Power Take-Off Tool

Set a goal or objective, such as Pat and Terry collaborating on the new business prospect of Pat's. Use this exercise to walk yourself through the power thinker process. This will help you consider new possibilities and alternatives you might not have otherwise considered. Review the facing page for more information.

Goal or Objective:

| |
| |

Plans: As you list out your activities below, think about the skills needed and the value the activities create.

Learn: What do you need to learn?	Skills Needed	Value Created
Think: What else do you need to think about?		
Act: What specific actions will you take?		
Accelerate: How will these activities above accelerate the achievement of your goal?		
Resources: Who or what can be a resource to help you achieve your goal?		

Ask Yourself

⇒ Who did you create value for today?

Ask Yourself

⇒ What is your primary thinking strategy? What comes to mind as you think about yourself, your clients and your resources relative to creating value?

⇒ When is the best time for you to take time and focus on creating value for your prospects and clients?

⇒ What is one thing you have done in the past week to create value for a prospect or client?

⇒ What stops you from planning?

⇒ What stops you from acting on your plan?

Chapter 2.4

Becoming a Value Creator Today
Crossing Your Success Gap

Quick Review on What You Have Accomplished with ZFactor

Congratulations. You've been encouraged to:

1. Develop some basic self-coaching skills;

2. Establish better and more consistent work habits, disciplines and behaviors, and stopped doing what doesn't make you money;

3. Identify your *Starting and Target Quadrants* on the *Sales Growth ZMap*;

4. Gain deeper understanding about who and where you are and who and where you want to be;

5. Learn to focus on specific sales skills and business practices to create greater value for your clients.

What's Next: Crossing Your Success Gap

A gap exists between your current performance and your ultimate objective to be a Partner and Value Creator. We refer to this gap as your *Success Gap*. As you move into *Part Three* to review the *Defining Characteristics* of successful sales professionals, you will reflect on the gaps between how you do business now and where you want to be as a successful sales professional.

All the work you have done throughout the book has been designed to help you complete this next section. This chapter reviews how to develop a plan for bridging your *Success Gap by* using the *Defining Characteristics* of Top Producers.

Consider a coach, mentor or respected peer to hold you accountable. It does make a difference.

Successful People Make More Money...But There's More To It...

Becoming a *Partner and Value Creator* has a greater purpose than just making more money. Yet, many define success in terms of income, sales, volume or profit. An authentic *Value Creator* includes the value their services provide clients as part of the work they do in their profession. For the *Partner and Value Creator* it becomes about making a difference in the lives of their co-workers and clients. Earning a large income is a result of taking exceptional care of all the people they come in contact with in their life. There is nothing wrong with being a *Value Creator* and making a lot of money, especially when your success is a result of others achieving their goals and dreams, as well.

As you think through how you will cross the various success gaps that exist on the road to becoming a *Partner and Value Creator*, you will recognize gaps that may involve different practices, techniques, processes, behaviors or disciplines. In fact, before crossing or closing these gaps, it will be necessary for you to successfully build a bridge to cross a specific *Success Gap*.

First, make a realistic assessment for how challenging it will be for you to close these gaps. Second, consider how big the gap is from your *Starting Quadrant* to your *Target Quadrant*. What are your scores? Do you have high scores or low scores? The lower the scores, the bigger the gap. Is your gap *Small, Challenging* or *Requires Significant Work*?

How Big is Your Success Gap?

1. **Small:** You know what you need to do. You just need to do it. It's like having a bridge already built that you can easily walk across. You have the required knowledge, experience, skills and resources. You know where you are and where you want to be. This requires a minor shift in thinking and perhaps a greater focus on disciplines. If you take the right actions you will easily get across the gap. It could be as easy as stop doing what doesn't work and do what you know works.

"Every man is guilty of all the good he didn't do."

~ Voltaire ~

2. **Challenging:** You may or may not know what to do. You may have some things to learn or need to find and engage necessary people and resources. In this case, imagine you have to build the bridge to get across. You need to access specific expertise in order to develop the plan to build the bridge. You need to develop or gain access to specific knowledge, experience, skills or resources in order to cross the gap. This requires very different thinking, clear and determined planning, time and focused attention—potentially an investment of time and or dollars. It may also mean changing out systems and processes to support a new efficiency in what you are trying to accomplish. Establish what to do and create a clear plan of action to cross the gap.

"We are all capable of much more than we think we are."

~ Lao Tzu ~

3. **Requires Significant Work:** You know the direction you want to go, but there is a lot of knowledge, skills, experience or time needed to make it happen. The gap is so large, you have to find a new way and/or find the necessary help or resources to cross the gap. This requires significant changes in your mindset and behavior and potentially even your entire work environment. It takes a warrior spirit with an intense focus on achieving your dreams. You have to be clear about where you are and understand more about where you want to be. The investment you make in yourself and your business will have significant returns. It's easy to get stuck in—*it will happen one day* thinking here—*one day* you will make the changes. Notice how time flies by as you drift along without striving to reach milestones. You've heard the song *"Turn Around…"*. One day you wake up and wonder where all the time went. Just do it, now!

Getting Started

As you work to plan and take the actions to *"Cross your Success Gap"* remember each *Success Gap* is the gap between your *Starting* and *Target Quadrants*. There will be other minor gaps identified as one works through the *Defining Characteristics* in Part Three. Ask Yourself questions are provided for each quadrant to help you focus on what to *Learn, Think, Act, and Accelerate* for planning purposes.

Do what Value Creators do. Keep doing those things, always getting better at what you do. Be patient. You will be recognized, someday.

The objective is to identify the gaps, resources required, and priorities for taking action to bridge the gaps. Some of these gaps can appear quite daunting at first, but if you *chunk down the* actions into areas that can be acted on by either current or acquired resources you will keep the momentum going along the backward *Z* in the ZMap.

For example, Pat thought to collaborate with Terry for meeting with the procurement person, because Pat knew he did not have the knowledge or skills to conduct a meeting on his own. This is a simple example of thinking and acting differently, yet very meaningful for the future growth of Pat's business. One has to set their ego aside in these situations, trusting that enlisting others so as to experience superior and effective interactions within sales situations will yield significant information. By reflecting on and assimilating new knowledge based on these observations, one can create the foundation for growth and development and eventually self sufficiency each step along the way.

As you are completing these steps, continue to keep the concept of *Partner and Value Creator* in mind. You want to understand how the actions you take today will create value for your clients now and into the future. While you may not be a fully developed Partner to your clients, you can still create value for others, today. Remember it takes discipline and practice, practice, practice…

Think of it as if you are planning a trip and you have your destination in mind. For example, you are in Houston and you want to go to New York. The distance between Houston and New York is similar to your *Success Gap*. As you embark upon the journey, you may discover alternate routes and various sights you want to see or events you want to attend. You may have to ask for directions. There are stops you have to make such as to get fuel and check the map. You don't change your ultimate destination, but you find various opportunities to enrich your journey with improvements to make it a better experience for you and others.

Start practicing today. No matter what quadrant you are starting in, you are offered multiple opportunities each day to think and act like a *Value Creator*. The authentic sales professional is all about seeking ways to enrich the lives of others through acts of significance. In every activity there is the seed of this type of contribution and value shows up where you choose to take one more step, ask one more question, make one more call, take a little extra time to review and be prepared, or review the details one more time. Practice the attitude of excellence and make everything important as it pertains to communicating and serving your clients. Maintain an attitude of greatness in everything you do.

At the end of each chapter in *Part Three*, you will find a template that will guide you to identify current gaps and associated actions you will take to bridge them.

Maintain an attitude of excellence in all aspects of life and business. You will attract the right people who want to work with you.

PART THREE

THE (Z) FACTOR

DEFINING CHARACTERISTICS

Part Three
Embrace the Defining Characteristics
Introduction

Defining Characteristics

All sales related information in this book has been compiled, tested and reviewed by sales professionals who have decades of sales and sales management achievements.

Change is an adventure and creates exciting experiences, especially for one committed to being a top sales producer. The sales profession offers the remarkable option to control your own destiny.

The *Defining Characteristics* in Part Three are focused on the attributes of professionals who are tasked with selling products. While the type of product and the length of the sales cycle will vary, it won't matter with the methodology. You can easily customize the ZMap experience to fit your situation, current skills and objectives. For professionals who sell *service-oriented* products (or even services), you can read in between the lines and substitute your common lingo to mold the methodology to fit your arena.

These characteristics have been reviewed and tested by professionals with decades of achievement and success. As you review these characteristics, be honest with yourself and evaluate how your sales practices and business activities compare. If you don't think you can be brutally honest with yourself, share these characteristics with someone you trust. Let them help you compare your performance to that of top producers. Hint: if you involve someone else in this activity, this clearly demonstrates your commitment to improve your performance.

Commit to Personal Excellence vs. Proving You are Better than Others

Becoming a *Value Creator* means clients no longer think of asking anyone else for similar products or services. The *Value Creator* no longer has to focus so intently on recreating new relationships, because clients know to call them when opportunities and challenges in business arise. The *Value Creator* has no competition. They are the competition. The contribution they make to clients is incredibly hard to duplicate (replace) and essential to day to day production of results (strategic initiatives) of their clients.

Successful people chose to make themselves a better professional.

Successful people who travel the top producer journey do not just start out with a silver spoon in their mouth. For those who achieve the *Value Creator* status, they earned the right to be there. Learning to make thinking a solid discipline is most of the battle. Surround yourself with good people and mentors. Plan your work and work you plan. Organize your thinking and your plans. Customize a ZMap to fit you, your skills, expertise and your unique situation.

You are encouraged to review all the characteristics in each quadrant and ask yourself how well you have developed each characteristic as it pertains to you and your business. These characteristics have been selected based on where mastery of them has increased sales productivity and/or created value for the clients of top producers. Successful professionals know how their business practices have been transformed because they chose to make themselves a better professional and be in service to their clients— rather than compare themselves to or try to prove they are better than other sales professionals in their industry.

Your Thinking Journey: A Roadmap of Defining Characteristics

The design of ZFactor allows you to adapt and change the *Defining Characteristics* to fit your *current* situation. And so, this methodology is designed to be revisited at least bi-annually and will continue to allow your thinking to evolve as do your disciplines, behaviors and results.

As you read through the *Defining Characteristics*, you may find, just as on a road trip, you have already visited a specific location. Some parts may feel like *been there, already done that*. It is recommended you simply be honest with yourself, and take the time to make sure you have not only *done it,* but you have it mastered! Remember this is about making yourself better at what you do—it's about excellence in practice. Not just running through the process in order to check the box. Set your mind, create the mindset to make it happen, for yourself, your family and your clients.

Be curious about the untapped potential awaiting you as you review and integrate these *Defining Characteristics* into your daily business

---

Ask Yourself

⇒ If you don't help find a way to create value for prospects and clients, who will?

---

practices. This is your opportunity to dive deeper and reveal the various gaps that may be stopping you from achieving your goals.

The objective is to help you decide how to prepare for the journey and which route to take. A general direction and plan has already been set and you are ready to venture on the road to your first destination—your *Target Quadrant*. You are provided a variety of concepts, practices and actions, all tested and proven by highly successful professionals.

We encourage you to embrace your *Warrior Spirit* and hurl yourself into this exciting adventure with the expectation you will release untapped potential for creating value for others.

Instructions for *Diving Deeper* into each Quadrant

There are four steps to complete in *Part Three*.

- **Read each Defining Characteristic:** Ask yourself how you would rank or compare your development and performance to a specific *Defining Characteristic*. Be your own coach, hire a coach, and/or review with a peer. You can use the suggested ranking process.

- **Rank yourself:** As you read each of the *Defining Characteristics*, rank yourself using a scale of 1 to 10 with 1 being limited competence and 10 being highly competent. A column is provided to the right of the Defining Characteristics for you to place your rank.

- **Ask Yourself:** Review and reflect on the *Ask Yourself* questions provided for each quadrant.

- **Create the Plan for Crossing the Gaps:** Use the *Crossing the Gap Action Planner* to help you focus of the *Defining Characteristics* you want to develop within yourself. A template is provided for each quadrant. You can copy these pages and use time and again.

Part Three Chapters are organized as follows:

- Overview of each Quadrant.

- A *Mostly True Story*: All the details are true in these stories, however, the names are clues to actual sales professionals and some

---

Ask Yourself

⇒ Are you curious to know your untapped potential?

⇒ How will you know you have achieved your potential?

Part Three is a ready made game plan for you to use with a coach or study group.

of the details are an amalgamation of several sales situations so as to demonstrate the point. This showcases how putting the defining characteristics into practice has accelerated success.

- Defining Characteristics of the Quadrant.

- Ask Yourself Questions.

- Crossing the Gap Action Planner.

The *Value Creator* has no competition. They are the competition.

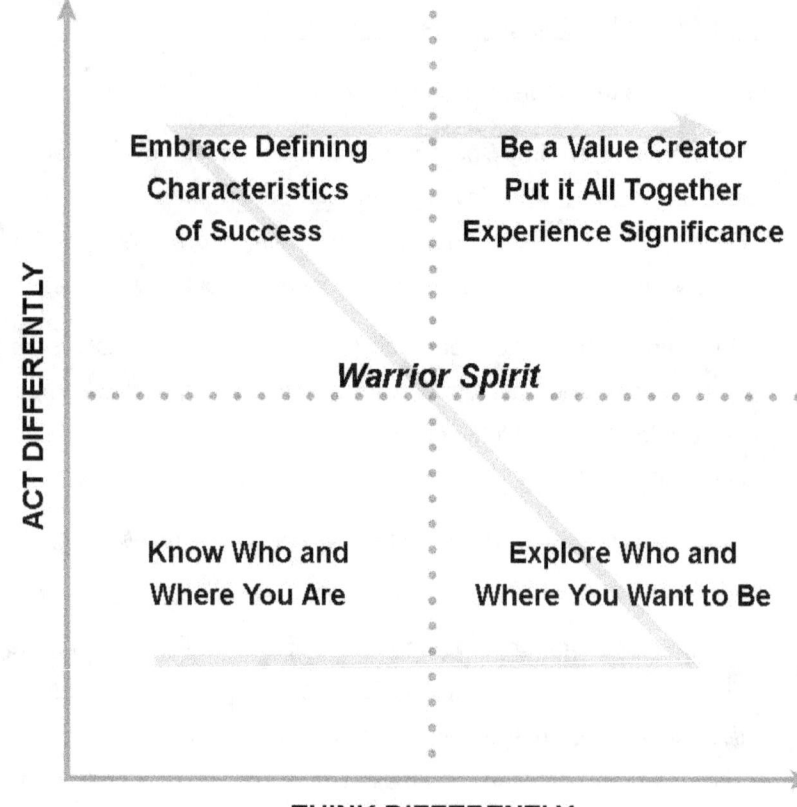

ZFactor Sales Accelerator

Embrace Defining Characteristics of Success

Be a Value Creator Put it All Together Experience Significance

Warrior Spirit

Know Who and Where You Are

Explore Who and Where You Want to Be

ACT DIFFERENTLY

THINK DIFFERENTLY

This ZMap provides a brief summary of the *Defining Characteristics* in each quadrant.

As you continually develop professional competencies, you will experience an acceleration in your performance.

Chapter 3.3 - Program Mastery

- **Continuous Learning**
  - Study business processes of your target clients.

- **Self-Management**
  - Focus only on ROR tasks first (return of revenue).

- **Planning**
  - Add planning and development of your team to your goals and projections.

- **Sales and Marketing**
  - Go after share of wallet and budgets (vs. sole buyers).

Chapter 3.4 - Value Creator

- **Continuous Learning**
  - Become an expert in your target clients' industry verticals.

- **Self-Management**
  - Create a work environment to support proactive and strategic focus on clients.

- **Planning**
  - Know the life-time value of client relationships and work a 3 year plan.

- **Sales and Marketing**
  - Refine leadership skills in community and industry.

Chapter 3.1 - Product Basics

- **Continuous Learning**
  - Be competent in a portfolio of products.

- **Self-Management**
  - Be disciplined and organized in all activities.

- **Planning**
  - Keep a simple To Do, Stop Do, Who Do list.

- **Sales and Marketing**
  - Match portfolio of products with target market.

Chapter 3.2 - Preferred Status

- **Continuous Learning**
  - Get training on tools, resources, communication and presentation skills.

- **Self-Management**
  - Clarify your values, beliefs, attitudes, behavior .

- **Planning**
  - Focus on client relationships to develop.

- **Sales and Marketing**
  - Establish consistent sales practices and processes.

SALES PERFORMANCE

PROFESSIONAL COMPETENCIES

Chapter 3.1

Quadrant 1: Product Basics

Product Knowledge and Sales Basics

Defining Characteristics

Overview of Product Basics for the Vendor Quadrant

Every journey has a definitive starting point and every professional has to know the basics about products, sales skills and business practices. We must have professional disciplines and good work habits to even have a chance to be successful. You might consider this the *Competence* quadrant, because the cornerstone for all success is competence related to your products and business model. You must know who you are, where you are, where you want to go and who you have to become to get where you want to be.

The most common motivator for entering sales is money. The second most common motivation is autonomy, which provides the freedom to be your own boss and have time to do the things you enjoy doing. Every successful salesperson has learned to be disciplined with their time and work habits to make the money they want. Successful people establish the right work habits and sales practices. Once Product Basics are mastered, one gains a deeper appreciation for interrelationship between the science and art of the sales profession. It is by investing time to develop highly effective sales skills that you experience the rewarding and fulfilling aspect of helping clients accomplish their goals in business.

Sales skills are not just a group of techniques and *How Tos* to convince someone to buy from you. Sales skills, as referred to in ZFactor, involve a complex process of learning and understanding the refined habits, disciplines, attitudes and behaviors that allow a prospect to understand and appreciate the value of the products and services offered by you.

The only limiting factor in the sales profession is you. No matter the economy, government regulations, company rules or personal situation there will always be the sales professional who achieves success.

Product Basics: You know who you are and what you sell. You are disciplined and competent with understanding of your available resources.

How you decide to prepare for the journey and which route you decide to take is entirely up to you. It's more fun to be with people you enjoy and they enjoy you.

Product Basics sounds easy and simple, doesn't it? Well, it might be simple, but it is not easy. It requires diligence, perseverance, and commitment. It is the foundation of your entire career. All top producers have not only mastered the basics but they continue to build their businesses on that solid foundation.

Product Basics for the Vendor: A Mostly True Story

Synopsis of Story

- **Background:** This story is about a sales professional who is a master at getting appointments through referrals and very innovative in his approach to selling product.

- **Situation:** Pete invested in sales training courses and learned to use questions in an interview setting to have a better understanding of what would provide value to the client. He is also a student of the ZFactor Methodology. This story is about a first meeting with a prospect and how Pete interviewed the client in such a way so as to have an opportunity to quote on projects. His long term goal was to replace the competition.

- **Result:** Pete had the opportunity to provide initial quotes on projects and eventually proved to provide more value to the client. As a result, his services became hard to replace and he won the right to manage all product sales with that client—replacing the original vendor who had the business.

Do you really believe sales is a noble profession? Believe it and achieve more than you can imagine.

I've had the opportunity to work with literally hundreds of sales professionals over my career. In a matter of moments I can usually tell where they were coming from when they share a story of a past meeting or their thinking about preparing for or an upcoming client interaction. One of the toughest spots for a sales professional is being pigeon-holed as merely a *product vendor* (and this can happen to even the most seasoned of folks). Products and services are commoditized, thus creating continuous competition in bidding situations to gain market share. Gross margins suffer as business is *bought* for the cash flow. Unfortunately, cash flow does not always translate into there being enough gross profit to cover costs!

All professionals have to master these basic understandings for the business of sales. They must learn the product set and the mechanics of getting sales through the system. Any professional can quickly grasp these basics as long as they have the right disciplines. Even the Top Producer starts here when they join a new company, switch their daily activities or add new products to their portfolio.

This story is about a sales professional who was referred to a new client contact by a neighbor. Interestingly, I have noticed a lot more referrals being generated by the 30-something generation. As they grow into positions of status, their relationships from school, college and earlier jobs are easily reignited through various social networks. The 30-somethings and 40-somethings are now becoming mature decision makers and the strength of using networks to reach referrals cannot be underestimated. With LinkedIn and Facebook, and other social mediums—it's a no-brainer these days.

To that end, one of the things Pete has always done well is network and leverage his existing relationships to open up doors. In this instance he was provided an executive's name, who then referred Pete *down* to the manager responsible for actually buying the type of products Pete sells.

Any sales professional can relate. The inside person is following the instructions of a higher up. While they are being *respectful* or nice, they usually have a relationship to whom they are loyal. The best opportunity one gets is a *chance to bid on the next project*—which the prospect of course will share with the current relationship so they can place an *informed* counter bid. This is exactly what happened. As a result, Pete was not being successful, because he was out bid every time by the incumbent.

It's great when *you* are the professional on the loyalty side of things of course, but beware! Be very aware when you are given another vendor's quotes to counter. This should be cause for concern, as you have actually backtracked in perceived service (your client is accepting other bids) and your business will, at some time, be at risk.

Pete knows this game. He has been on both sides of the table, as a new bidder and the incumbent. He knew it was time for new thinking and new actions. Seeing this opportunity, he pushed for an appointment prior to getting the *next bid opportunity* email. He knew this might be his only

> Product Basics are like air and water. You cannot exist very long without them. If you ignore them, your sales die.

opportunity to reframe the client's perception of who he was and what value he could provide to the company—beyond just price. He knew that moving from being just another vendor to having more mindshare with the client required understanding the client's situation in further detail.

He did get the meeting, and got the *spiel* on how important price is and that they had a current vendor who provided them good pricing. Pete listened and then asked, "So knowing that clients want all three things—a good price, quality (getting it right) and timely responses and delivery—can you tell me about what you have in place, now and what you'd like to have that maybe you don't have today?"

A co-worker of the prospect had joined the meeting and started talking. Pete asked for specific examples and it quickly became clear that while the pricing was competitive with their current vendor, there were issues with customer service and in particular with responsiveness and communication. Pete listened and soaked it in.

At the appropriate moment, Pete talked about his team and approach to serving clients. He focused at a very high level on the process and systems in place that made a difference for customer service, communication and response time. He then asked further questions to gain better understanding of the prospect's needs. He explained how he and his team actually make themselves an extension of the client's team.

Pete was clear he no longer wanted to be just another order taker. He was positioning to be irreplaceable. And then he asked (more like stated), "So if we got orders right with delivery on time, and you knew the status all along the way—and we did that every time—wouldn't that be worth a few extra pennies? How much would that save you in time and hassle if nothing else?" As expected, they agreed it might be of value (but of course price was very important!). The prospect, being perfectly normal, was just doing it the way it's always been done. It had not occurred to them how cumbersome the current process was. It took Pete asking questions like a *Value Creator* to plant the seed of a better way.

A product *order taker* most likely would have pulled out a catalog at this point to get an order. Instead, Pete continued to ask questions, get a

Tired of being *just another vendor*!

You must be willing to do the work to make the change.

timeline of projects, find out the category types of products they had historically purchased, and made commitments on when he would provide a response to include some suggestions and ideas for upcoming events. Instead of receiving a bid request for specific products, he offered to propose new ideas for their consideration.

Pete earned an opportunity to start working with their business by uncovering where he could provide value. Of course the first orders were the most critical as he and his team learned how the client accepted communications and what that meant to all of them specifically. As he and his team moved into the *Preferred Status* quadrant with this client, he could then start finding out how to become more strategically involved with their business— and as such he is already putting in play the traits of the Value Creator.

Another Story...

I wasn't planning on putting another story in here, but felt compelled to add this one. This is the story of a young guy that sells what one might consider to be quite a mundane product, with minimal differentiating factors other than brand name—and one in which the market has literally hundreds of options for this particular product. Well...he doesn't actually sell them—he delivers these products. What is it? Pizza.

This job has a small base wage, but as you can imagine the *upside* and opportunity for income comes from tips. In sharing his story, Ken explained how he began to notice the response and reaction various people had to him when he approached their door with the promised pizzas. At 6'3", Ken carries quite a presence and can be a little intimidating to some of the customers he services.

Here is why his story is being included in this section. By noticing *how* he was being perceived, Ken began to change his approach and interaction with customers—based on who they appeared to be. He discovered that some had no interest in chit-chat and just wanted to complete the transaction ASAP. For some, it was best that he stand back from the door several feet, while for others, they might want to visit, ask about him, enjoy some humor or talk about sports and the college team. Whoop!

> **Ask Yourself**
>
> A client gives you another product order.
> ⇒ How do you plan to become a value creator for them?

There's real value to be realized when you put customers first and learn how they want to do business with you.

Over time he has gotten to know the customer type inclined to give him a bigger tip with a tailored approach. The result? He has repeat customers and has increased his weekly tips significantly. Even with a product like a pizza, one can find a way to leverage the buyer experience to create a situation for being hard to replace with your customer. Yes, one can take pride and work with an attitude of excellence even delivering pizzas in a college town! Ken started thinking and acting differently and increased his tips.

Product Basics—Defining Characteristics

1. **Continuous Learning:** Be competent in a portfolio of products.
2. **Self-Management:** Be disciplined and organized in all activities.
3. **Planning:** Keep a simple To Do, Stop Do, Who Do list.
4. **Sales and Marketing:** Match portfolio of products with target market.

	Rank each statement on a scale of 1 to 10. 1 is limited competence. 10 is highly competent.	Rank
Learn	• I am competent in selling a portfolio of products and know which sources and sales approaches meet the needs of my target clients. • I establish good time and contact management practices and have applied the best organizational skills to fit me and my business activities. • I continually read new materials provided to me by my company and books on sales, human behavior and industry news, all for development and improvement. • I learn how to prospect for people who have needs that match my product knowledge and approach to service. • I am committed to learning what successful people do, no matter what.	
Think	• I believe in myself and am very clear about why I am in this business. • I prepare myself for meetings with prospects by preparing and anticipating questions. • I think about each interview at the conclusion of each meeting and record my thoughts about how I might improve my process. • I feed my mind with inspiring stories that stimulate thinking and desire to achieve excellence.	
Act	• I maintain an active 'To Do' and 'Stop Do' list. • I have developed and work a simple sales presentation based on a needs analysis approach. • I continue to refine my knowledge and apply it to identify prospects that have a basic need for my full product and service offering.	
Accelerate	• I demonstrate interest in my clients beyond just making the sale. • I select at least 20 current clients a week to make contact with. • I send short, handwritten thank you notes following interviews with a prospect or client. • I send articles of interest to every prospect or client as I think appropriate. • I send cards and notes to clients for special family and personal events and occasions.	

Ask Yourself

Review these questions to clarify, for yourself, how you compare to a top producer. Consider how a top producer might answer these questions. Then what is the reality for yourself?

Continuous Learning	• What are you doing to be competent in a portfolio of products? • What level of commitment and investment in time and money do you devote to improving your sales knowledge and skills?
Self-Management	• How committed are you to personal and professional development when considering how much money and time is being spent? • On a scale of 1 to 10, how would you rate your commitment and effectiveness in self-discipline and in organizing all activities?
Planning	• What is one item on your To Do list or Stop Do list you just don't get done? • On a scale of 1 to 10, rate your success at achieving your sales goals.
Sales and Marketing Skills	• Have you described, in writing, your target market and clients within that market? • Do you know which prospects you plan to contact each day?

Your Notes

Crossing the Gap Action Planner—from Product Basics to Preferred Status

1. Create Your Gap List

Consider the Defining Characteristics listed on page 105. Which characteristics do you need to improve in order to move yourself toward the Preferred Status quadrant? Write your answers here or in your journal for each gap identified. Start with no more than three gaps. Once you complete your initial gaps, you can work on others. Copy of this page permitted.

GAP: (write your specific gap here)	ANSWERS
What do you need to learn to help you cross this gap?	
How do you need to think differently about this gap or situation? Who might give you a different perspective to consider?	
How will what you learn change your mindset and accelerate you toward your objective?	
What are the types of actions you plan to take?	

2. Action Plan

What specific actions do you plan to take?

Based on the gaps identified in *Learn, Think, Act, Accelerate* on page 105, what are three to five specific actions you plan to take to improve your situation to cross the gap and move you toward your next quadrant? Reflect on these questions as you set your actions into motion.

- How will these actions make you *Hard to Replace*?
- How will these actions increase the quantity and quality of your client relationships?
- How will you know you have mastered this quadrant?

My Planned Actions	Start Date	Complete Date

Chapter 3.2

Quadrant 2: Preferred Status

Building Relationships for Consistent Referrals

Defining Characteristics

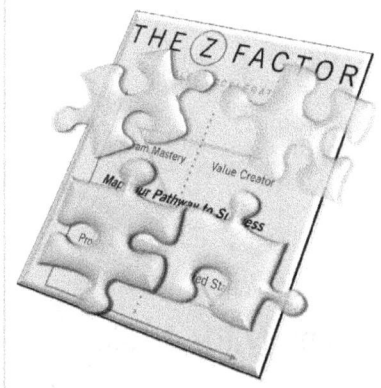

Overview of Preferred Status Quadrant

As the professional gains experience with clients, they learn to integrate who they are with their business practices and continue developing disciplines to support growth and repeatable business. Personal and professional knowledge, interests, values, experiences, and talents are developed into a consistent sales system, which is continually refined and improved throughout their career. Through this process, the professional establishes methods for attaining *preferred vendor status* (either formally or informally) and leverages these relationships to create a solid referral strategy that produces sustainable results. One can consider this the *Confidence* quadrant because the sales professional learns who the best clients are and implements strategies and consistent processes for acquiring and retaining their ideal clients. Here the client might say something like, "*I don't know what I'd do without you.*"

There are some sales professionals with many years of experience, who have merely repeated their first year experience over and over again every year. They just keep doing the same thing again and again, always hoping something will change. This is the source of the old expression, *one year's experience repeated twenty times*. To gain mastery in this quadrant is to put in place the *machine* that produces specific outcomes for the acquisition, development and retention of customers. The primary goals to achieve *Preferred Status* are to:

- Establish an organizational structure (people, process, platform) that produces a sound and efficient process for managing the full order lifecycle such that you move out of order administration and into order *origination*;

- Adhere to a plan that begins with annualized goals and breaks down by quarter into monthly and weekly goals (for acquisition, development and retention to drive success).

Preferred Status: You have integrated who you are into a consistent sales system and are continually improving. You have become a preferred vendor which increases your Confidence to work with only your best and most profitable clients.

Preferred vendor status is quite an achievement. This requires solid relationships. Only, people change jobs and someone always has a lower price.

You are over half way to Value Creator. What's next?

Keep on practicing and learning. Mastery is simply the basics with very different and unique thoughts put into action with the confidence you can make a difference.

- Discipline your time so that *profit-making* activities do not get side-lined by administrative and follow-up activities. This means you have to block time and keep to it, setting aside a reactive nature and replacing it with proactive habits;

- Implement a robust relationship management and referral program that has a continuous feed of opportunities for your pipeline so you can expand and grow existing customers, develop them into preferred relationships and find new ones that fit your ideal target customer profile.

Finally, essential to success for growing your business and any major opportunity is a *Champion.* A Champion is a buying customer who encourages others in their company to buy from you as well. The key is they have three essential attributes that allow you to leverage this relationship to new levels. They have *responsibility, influence, and authority* over purchasing from you and ultimately at an organizational level, as well.

Preferred Status: A Mostly True Story

Synopsis of Story

- **Background:** This story is about a sales professional who knew the mechanics of how to become established as a preferred vendor with her target clients. She knew changes in her overall approach were needed as a result of developments with a key client.

- **Situation:** Robyn had positioned to be a preferred vendor for a major client. However, she soon found she didn't have a true Champion that could ensure purchasing by other buyers.

- **Result:** Robyn leveraged her position as a preferred vendor and found ways to strategically engage a true Champion to work with her to gain market share within a new customer opportunity.

Robyn had been selling for about 8 years and had mastered an understanding of how to meet client's needs with her product sources and solutions. She had been fairly successful in filling the forms and following the processes for being acknowledged as a preferred vendor for several clients.

Challenged by the loss of significant revenue from a major client (through a RFP process that narrowed vendors into specific categories and locked down any other sales options) she had to evaluate where to rebuild. Ironically, the RFP process with that client awarded her *preferred vendor status*, but in actuality the client's program forced her to be classified in the Product Basics quadrant. This was because the company had multiple vendors competing in the same category and her offering was viewed as just a commodity—and thus deemed easy to replace and unimportant strategically to the company.

Robyn had to learn this the hard way, losing six figures in revenue practically overnight. While the primary relationships at her client had responsibility for purchasing from her and influence over the process (they got her in the RFP process after all) they had NO *authority* over the preferred vendor selection or in getting others to buy from her. Therefore, she did not have a *true* Champion at that client. All three attributes (*responsibility*, *influence*, *and authority*) must exist for the ideal situation to reveal itself.

So, Robyn focused on finding a true Champion this time and soon met Hank, who worked at another client of hers. Robyn knew while she was starting with a minimal amount of business with this client, there was a huge opportunity to expand the business if she could leverage this relationship.

Starting with this one relationship, she grew to understand the structure of the entire organization with the help of her Champion. Hank began introducing Robyn to others in both the marketing and procurement functions of the organization. Over the course of a year, she began to treat this organization as a whole system and communicate in such a way that a buying *community* began to develop within this account. By doing this, she began to set this client up for advancement to our next quadrant, *Program Mastery* (more on that later).

The important thing to understand here is Robyn had a clearly defined plan for how to make this happen and her Champion, Hank, was a true collaborator with her every step of the way. Together, they boldly pushed for a first time contract that would consolidate product and process activities across all functional areas. As a result, she was able to leverage technology

Ask Yourself

Losing revenue is painful.

⇒ Are you working with clients who have these three attributes?

1. Responsibility
2. Influence
3. Authority

to streamline ordering and communication and put standards in place that became very difficult to replace.

Robyn's focus was always from her Champion's perspective, his needs and what would make him shine in his role. She leveraged this influence to make the Champion look great, while offering up new solutions for operating their business. This made Robyn invaluable in terms of responsiveness and service. She went from one buyer, her Champion, to over 30 across the nation and grew the program from four zeros to over six zeros in the course of just one year.

Put yourself in your Champion's shoes. Meet their needs and make them shine!

Preferred Status—Defining Characteristics

1. **Continuous Learning:** Get training on tools, resources, communication and presentation skills.
2. **Self-Management:** Clarify your values, beliefs, attitudes and behavior.
3. **Planning:** Focus on the right client relationships to develop.
4. **Sales and Marketing:** Establish consistent sales practices and processes.

	Rank each statement on a scale of 1 to 10. 1 is limited competence. 10 is highly competent.	Rank
Learn	• I learn how my client and their company make decisions for assigning preferred vendor status. • I participate in training on tools and techniques for my products and discover the keys to effective communication that build trust and add value to relationships. • I observe and listen for how clients and prospects respond to questions. • I find out if my buyers and those around them have responsibility, influence and authority over decisions. If so, I begin to cultivate those relationships or find the one's that do.	
Think	• I reflect on my attempts to build solid relationships with clients and refine what I do to develop systems that support my being afforded all opportunities as a preferred vendor. • I study the top producers in my field and think about how to apply new ideas to be hard to replace with my clients. • I have written out my objectives and goals. I know what I want to achieve with my client relationships. I keep my actions aligned with my plans.	
Act	• I have developed an interview sales process to help gather pertinent information to help me understand more about pain points and process challenges for my client's needs or problems. • I use a consultative approach to focus on planning-oriented solutions rather than single product sales. • I organize my activities around the need to be in front of qualified prospects and clients. I am clear when I make referral requests for my Ideal Client. • I keep detailed records of the results of my activities.	
Accelerate	• I have developed a one-page Ideal Client Profile, based on the characteristics of my top clients. I use this tool for identifying qualified prospective new clients. • I meet with my top clients at least once a quarter and let them know I value their assistance in recommending me to their friends, family, and colleagues. I ask for referrals to my Ideal Clients. • I contact the top 20% of my clients on a regular basis to update them on any new events and ask about their activities. • I manage my social network online and in person to further nurture these relationships. • I stay on the lookout for Champions and cultivate relationships over time, never knowing when an acquaintance, former co-worker, friend from college may be promoted to Champion status.	

Ask Yourself

Review these questions to clarify, for yourself, how you compare to a top producer. Consider how a top producer might answer these questions. Then what is the reality for yourself?

Continuous Learning	• How are you expanding your knowledge, skills, and ability for being qualified as a preferred vendor? • What is your process for learning to be more effective in your consultative approach to determine the concerns and needs of your clients? • What training do you need to take to improve your knowledge of products, or improve your communication and presentation skills?
Self-Management	• What metrics are you using to measure performance against your goals? • How do you track your time and activities to hold yourself accountable for strategy execution? • What process do you have for reflecting on your values, beliefs and results?
Planning	• What is your planned schedule for client contact, reviews, and follow-up? • How effective is your scheduled touch-point process? Is it providing the level of results you expect for growth and maintaining the level of service you promise to your clients? • How will you approach improving the *quality* of your client relationships?
Sales and Marketing Skills	• Have you created an Ideal Client Profile to use in asking for referrals and personal introductions to qualified prospective clients? • Have you segmented your book of business to identify your top clients? Do you use that information to deliver targeted relationship building strategies to those "A" level clients?

Your Notes

Crossing the Gap Action Planner—from Preferred Status to Program Mastery

1. Create Your Gap List

Consider the Defining Characteristics listed on page 113. Which characteristics do you need to improve in order to move yourself toward the Preferred Status quadrant? Write your answers here or in your journal for each gap identified. Start with no more than three gaps. Once you complete your initial gaps, you can work on others. Copy of this page permitted.

GAP: (write your specific gap here)	ANSWERS
What do you need to learn to help you cross this gap?	
How do you need to think differently about this gap or situation? Who might give you a different perspective to consider?	
How will what you learn change your mindset and accelerate you toward your objective?	
What are the types of actions you plan to take?	

2. Action Plan

What specific actions do you plan to take?

Based on the gaps identified in *Learn, Think, Act, Accelerate* on page 113, what is one or more action you plan to take to improve your situation and move you toward your next quadrant?

- How will these actions make you *Strategically Important*?

- How will these actions increase your understanding of your clients' situations and business needs?

- How will you know you have mastered this quadrant?

My Planned Actions	Start Date	Complete Date

Chapter 3.3

Quadrant 3: Program Mastery

Becoming Strategically Important

Defining Characteristics

Overview Program Mastery Quadrant

In the early days of being in the business, we often feel as though we are unemployed every morning unless we have an appointment with a client or prospective new client. Gradually, this passes and we experience success. Program Mastery is the result of the accumulation of experience, knowledge and application of expertise in a specific niche with a client—or perhaps with an industry vertical where you can duplicate a program several times over. Top Producers are not *jacks of all trades*—they are specialists. They have transmuted themselves and business activities into a mastery of sales, systems, planning, processes, people and business development.

What separates the top producer from the average producer? The top producer continues to invest in learning and developing themselves personally and professionally. Everything they learned in Product Basics quadrant and Preferred Status quadrants now is applied to create the foundation for building a sustainable and successful business. Their untapped potential for business success is released. They have become more than just another sales professional. The focus now is on integrating product and process solutions into an approach that solves problems and serves a specific purpose—often more strategic in design. This quadrant is considered the *Communicator* quadrant, because relationships within the ideal client move from selling 1:1 to serving groups or departments to deliver more complex results (often integrated across the enterprise). Here the client might say something like, "*I don't know what **we** would do without you.*"

In the prior story I referenced how Robyn had decided to secure a contract as part of the strategy for growing the account. This may or may not be necessary for all client situations (or even a valid tactic), but some form of agreement—formal or not—must be in place prior to investing the time and

Program Mastery: You continue to invest into yourself and your business, especially as it relates to your presentation and Communication skills. You are building a sustainable, successful business by delivering solutions for managing complex client situations.

Top Producers are always learning and developing themselves personally and professionally.

This has a high ROTI (Return on Time Invested).

resources into becoming a program master with your client. The goal is to thoroughly understand and review the current relationship to confirm the structure and solution that can be put in place to leverage your services for a specific area of the business or across the enterprise.

Program, simply defined—*your role is a strategic element of the client's business initiatives.*

A program, simply defined, is anywhere your offering is a strategic element of your client's overall business initiatives in one or more areas. Within a program you interface with people to offer process-oriented methods for product delivery—often leveraging technology (but not always). You are solving a problem that the client in essence outsources to you. Thus your program is an extension of their business—and when crafted masterfully becomes strategically important to their day to day delivery on their business objectives. In summary:

- Secure agreement with a Champion (or multiple Champions) who has committed to you and has a vested interest in the mutual success of the program;

- Understand the results the client is trying to produce through the use of your product solutions so you see the pain points and road blocks the client is experiencing;

- Evaluate where you can become invaluable by saving time or performing services (process) in such a way that your role is *written* into the client's plan for how this unit or the company achieves their objectives;

- Determine where process and technology can be used to streamline communication, leverage activities and drive time and cost savings;

- Drive awareness of your services as the solution source, which begins when you become interwoven into the everyday practices—creating smiles—solving problems—improving the landscape for adoption of product and services.

Net is—you want to become an extension of your client's team and provide a solution that is strategically important to your client's business outcomes. Teach your client how to leverage you and your resources for their best interests. Mastery in this quadrant now integrates this understanding with the foundation you laid for them to trust your product quality and pricing *with* a proven perception that you are darn near impossible to replace because of what you offer. Remember, they are likely to say, *"I don't know what we'd do without you!"*

Program Mastery: A Mostly True Story

Synopsis of Story

- **Background:** This sales professional had a long-term working relationship with a loyal buyer and had grown to know a lot about his style of working. Zane also understood this client's professional goals for the division he was running and Zane was keenly aware of the challenges the client was facing.

- **Situation:** Zane's buyer was promoted to a position that gave him authority over an entire budget for a major division of the company. As a result, Zane's contact inherited multiple vendor relationships. He had responsibility for tracking and reporting on the entire divisional budget and now had to manage a variety of processes around ordering and distribution of products (essentially everyone had been buying however they wanted to and from whomever they chose).

- **Result:** Zane recognized that his contact was now a Champion, and as such had responsibility, influence and authority over the people, processes and platform (systems) for managing this area of purchasing in the company. Zane found the opportunity to move from Preferred Status into a leadership position with his Champion by providing strategic services as an extension of the client's team.

Zane had a loyal buyer that had been with him for over 7 years. In fact, in many ways they had grown up together as each had progressed in their talents and abilities in their respective positions. Eventually Zane's buyer (Al) went from just having responsibility for purchasing products to being a true Champion as he gained influence and authority over marketing for a geographic region of the company.

The evolving sales professionals continues to see the statue waiting to be revealed inside the block of stone.

Sometimes it takes a lot of chiseling so others see it, as well

As Al's responsibilities grew, so did the inefficiencies around how he was managing the purchase and distribution of products. Al had gone from managing just his budget to having responsibility for consolidating multiple budgets. This meant new vendors and new ordering processes because each former buyer had their own vendors and ways of doing things. Zane began to see he was only getting a portion of the overall business. Al was distributing his business to multiple vendors in an effort to grow his services to the field without having to add additional staff.

For almost a year, Zane continued to share information on additional services he could offer to save Al and his team time on the sourcing and distribution of his products. But, Al was always too busy to take time to consider a change. Finally, one day, Zane did a presentation *on the fly* in 5 minutes that hooked Al into understanding there might be a better way. (Actually, it looked like it was *on the fly*, but Zane had spent quite a bit of time thinking through and creating materials that would tell the story quickly).

Over the following months, Zane became immersed in understanding what Al was trying to accomplish and why. He spent time looking at the entire lifecycle of why his products were selected and where they ended up. Zane focused on the result that Al was trying to produce and leveraged the relationship to build trust and confidence with Al. Together they explored how development of their teams, refining processes and use of technology tools could substantially improve the program results overall. Both of them focused on how *all* activities would produce these results (and a return of revenue) for the time invested.

The result was that Zane helped Al eliminate several vendors and Zane eventually partnered with one other vendor to narrow down the solution to just two sources for meeting all of Al's needs. Zane became the lead on the program and the single source for his products for the entire division. Sales increased by 5 times in the first year of the program. The entire program began producing a measurable return and was included in annual budgeting as a strategic initiative for the entire region.

That's not the rest of the story—yet—as Al was recently promoted again, and Zane and Al have approval to expand the program to another (and larger) region of the company. Al's program was built and working—and solved

Masters have all the tools and relationships, and best of all, the vision and leadership to make it happen.

a problem that other regions were also struggling with. Thus their program was selected after a thorough review and comparison within the company of what other regions were doing.

Of note here, is that Zane had the aptitude and experience to take a consultative approach to servicing this client. Zane changed his thinking to that of a master artist. Instead of seeing only a block of granite, the master artist will envision the statue that is yet to be revealed and released from within the block of stone. Zane saw only the potential and produced a work of art, as a Program Master.

Many of the tasks Zane performed were not traditional sales and might be considered out of scope for this role—and one could indeed argue that point. However, if you want to exponentially increase revenues, then there must be a plan and intention to move from just selling Product, to being a Preferred resource, to selling into Program Mastery—which always involves understanding the strategic importance of your offering. The sales professional who has achieved the Program Mastery quadrant not only envisions the possibilities, but has developed their capabilities to make things happen when competitors can only wonder, how did they do that?

If you don't have these skills, yet—find someone within your organization (management or mentor) who does and can make it happen. Leverage your relationships and resources!

Formula to Increase Revenue

Know Yourself

Know Your Products

Know Your Client

Know Your Resources

Be a Program Master

Sustainable Revenue

Focus:

On relationships and revenue...all else follows.

Program Mastery—Defining Characteristics

1. **Continuous Learning:** Study business processes of your target clients.
2. **Self-Management:** Focus only on ROR tasks first (return of revenue).
3. **Planning:** Add planning and development of your team to your goals and projections.
4. **Sales and Marketing:** Go after share of wallet and budgets (vs. sole buyers).

	Rank each statement on a scale of 1 to 10. 1 is limited competence. 10 is highly competent.	Rank
Learn	• I read and study business oriented materials that help me understand process as it relates to my clients and their industries. • I study and gather information on industry verticals with specific problems my services address. • I read business books to learn more about building a sustainable business. I also seek out and learn the basics on business building from the masters. • I engage the services of a professional coach and/or mentor to learn from their experience.	
Think	• I think about my business systems and processes and refine them for maximum effectiveness. • I read and reflect on books, blogs, e-publications that cover sales, psychology, marketing, and business building on a regular basis. • I continuously ask myself, if I am clearly communicating the value of my expertise to those who can most appreciate my products and services.	
Act	• I develop practices, systems, and processes that improve my organizational skills and effectiveness. I make sure my action plans support the metrics of my tracking system. • I incorporate development of my team in goal setting and find areas where I must outsource activities that are not the best use of my time (low return of revenue for time invested). • I am prepared at any moment to show case scenarios that demonstrate the strategic value I offer to my clients. • I know what I am looking for in a Champion, and I am actively evaluating the organizational structure of the company. I know how buying is organized so I can grow the share of wallet I get from my clients. • I am actively reviewing the business initiatives of my top clients and *seeding* the conversations with them to open up doors for expansion of my business with them.	
Accelerate	• I have an organized and up to date Contact/Relationship Management System with essential information I need about what is of strategic importance to my clients (beyond just their contact data). This makes it so I can stay on top of my clients' needs. • I contact my top clients at least once per month without attempting to sell anything. I nurture these clients by demonstrating my willingness to fully engage and to serve their needs. • I advise my clients of ways I can save time or money for them either through service/process or technology-enabled collaboration with me. This may be as simple as email or as complex as a custom solution that integrates people, process and platform to achieve a specific outcome. • I show client appreciation by acknowledging significant events in their business or personal life.	

Ask Yourself

Review these questions to clarify, for yourself, how you compare to a top producer. Consider how a top producer might answer these questions. Then what is the reality for yourself?

Continuous Learning	• What is your commitment to and time frame for filling in your biggest knowledge gaps around an industry vertical, business processes and/or technology? • What is your process for continuously expanding your knowledge of advanced uses of your products and associated services in solving client's problems? • What is your process for understanding the strategic initiatives of your clients?
Self-Management	• How do you measure and track profitability of your business? • What professional organizations do you belong to and how do you contribute to your industry and community? How will you be viewed as an expert? • Are you tracking your time and your team's time and do you have a thorough knowledge of the most productive and highest revenue producing activities?
Planning	• How do your mission and value statements reflect your commitment to client development and providing unparalleled results for your clients? • What are your plans for personal and professional development and for leveraging the services of a professional coach or mentor? • Do you meet with clients on a quarterly basis to assess their plans for the immediate and long-term future?
Sales and Marketing Skills	• How effective is your referral process and does it demonstrate your commitment to professionalism? • How often do you review and revise your business plan, action plan, and target Client Profile? • How often do you review the segmenting of your book of business to further refine the characteristics of your top clients? • What are you doing to become a master at asking questions and specifically as they relate to the initiatives of your clients and the results they are seeking?

Your Notes

Crossing the Gap Action Planner—from Program Mastery to Value Creator

1. Create Your Gap List

Consider the Defining Characteristics listed on page 122. Which characteristics do you need to improve in order to move yourself toward the Preferred Status quadrant? Write your answers here or in your journal for each gap identified. Start with no more than three gaps. Once you complete your initial gaps, you can work on others. Copy of this page permitted.

GAP: (write your specific gap here)	ANSWERS
What do you need to learn to help you cross this gap?	
How do you need to think differently about this gap or situation? Who might give you a different perspective to consider?	
How will what you learn change your mindset and accelerate you toward your objective?	
What are the types of actions you plan to take?	

2. Action Plan

What specific actions do you plan to take?

Based on the gaps identified in *Learn, Think, Act, Accelerate* on page 122, what is one or more actions you plan to take to improve your situation and move you toward your next quadrant?

- How will these actions make you *Strategically Important* and *Hard to Replace*?
- How will these actions increase your understanding of your clients' situations and business needs?
- How will you know you have mastered this quadrant?

My Planned Actions	Start Date	Complete Date

Chapter 3.4

Quadrant 4: Value Creator

Journey into the Fourth Quadrant

Defining Characteristics

Partner and Value Creator

The pinnacle of business success, the Value Creator no longer depends on product to differentiate them with clients. The sales professional, as a Value Creator *is* the differentiating factor by providing a level of strategic value so interwoven into the fabric of the client's business that they are *irreplaceable*. A Value Creator has created a stable and sustainable business. They plan and project a lifetime value of their client base. They are the *Go To* expert and highly influential in the industry and local community. They are the role model others want to become because they have achieved a high level of financial success and a work-life balance of significance. The Value Creator distinction is earned only when one experiences recognition of this status from others. For their clients, the Value Creator is known as the *Catalyzer* and they bring all their talents to the client to collaborate, plan and deliver on producing innovative results. Here the client might say something like, "*I don't know what we did BEFORE you.*"

The amazing thing is the Value Creator has clients follow them wherever they go—and the client takes the Value Creator with them as they move on with their career. This type of relationship is ideal, because this client is not only a Champion, but they are a trusted business companion and in many cases a friend.

What does it take to attain this level of significance and how will you know when you have *arrived*? In reality, expect to always be *arriving*. There's always another mountain to climb and bigger fish to catch. It's in the blood. It's who they are. It's fun and fulfilling to make a difference—be significant.

One of the ways we demonstrate our value to others is by being truly authentic. We engage in relationships in a very personal way and it is clear

Partner and Value Creator: You have achieved the pinnacle of your career marked by the fact that you and your acquired expertise are the differentiating factor, not your products. You have become both strategically important and hard to replace with your ideal, favorable clients. You are considered a catalyzer in how you bring all talents and resources to the client to collaborate, plan and deliver innovative results.

Champions change jobs and move to new companies. They make things happen and bring those along who are essential for helping them make things happen.

When you can create value for others with no thought of any reward, you will live a life of significance beyond any of your imaginings.

to everyone that our agenda and motivation are in perfect alignment with who we are and the personal vision and values we represent. Selling our products and services remains the objective, but it is clear that the focus is on contributing to the personal and professional well being of clients.

Now imagine value as something way beyond great products, low-costs, or even excellent advice, service and plans. Envision a role where your contribution to your clients far surpasses the singular role of being a vendor to the company—where you are more than just on an approved list of preferred vendors. You are strategically a part of one or more business initiatives and have an intimate understanding of what the client is attempting to accomplish through the use of you, your products and services. This is what it means to be a *Value Creator*.

What do Value Creators have in common? They obviously think and act differently. But, how does that show up in what they do? There are six key elements that identify a Value Creator:

- They are self-competent, confident and fully engaged in seeing the world through the lens of the clients.

- They think in terms of solving problems and always place their clients' concerns ahead of their own.

- They behave in ways that exemplify integrity—personally, in business, and in their community.

- They take action based on the highest principles and practices and are professional in every respect.

- They believe in their own value, the value of their ideas and products, and the contribution they make to the benefit of others.

- They are leaders.

Many of those considered to be Value Creators, think in terms of their business as a calling. In that role it is not what they do so much as it is who *they are being when they do it*.

Value Creator: A Mostly True Story

Synopsis of Story

- **Background:** This sales professional made a career decision to completely transform the portfolio of clients she serviced in her overall book of business. Her goal was to convert from being a transaction oriented business to one with strategic plans for both her business and her clients.

- **Situation:** Georgia was a preferred vendor for many of her clients and had several programs with predictability and reoccurring revenue as a result. She had become very talented at looking for and listening to the strategic goals of her clients, but had only been successful at a regional or divisional level thus far. She set a 3 year strategic goal to expand targeted clients to the enterprise level so that she could build a team and be the exclusive provider of her products to a smaller base of clients with a more predictable base of sustainable, ongoing revenue.

- **Result**: Georgia put a plan in place and targeted existing clients for development and several new clients to acquire. Here are two stories on relationships and the progression of her development into becoming a Value Creator not only for her Champions—but also for their entire company. Please note that Georgia was already behaving like a Value Creator *before* she embarked on this transformation of her client base. It was because of her focus, hard work and a commitment to bridging the gaps between her current status, in the eye of the client, to the desired position of Value Creator that she was able to realize the untapped revenue potential within her client base.

I have been blessed to work with many Value Creators over my years in sales and sales leadership. It would be easy to think that age would have a significant impact on the status of Value Creator, but that is not always the case. While experience does play a factor, there are people who know how to accelerate learning by leveraging expert mentors. They can achieve as much in just one year where as it takes others many years to discover the

> Value… Meaning… Significance...
>
> Desire to make a difference and do all you can do. Others will measure the value of your life by what you mean to them, not by how much money you make.

Value Creators do the things value creators do—long before ever being recognized as a Value Creator.

Other Value Creators can see emerging Value Creators coming.

same thing. The exciting thing is when a sales professional makes the decision to transform their business and their life—the resulting value it offers them, their family, their team and their clients is extraordinary. A good sales manager/executive can SEE them coming. If management doesn't see or acknowledge them, these Value Creators move on and away, quickly.

Fortunately, I could see Georgia coming. For three years, Georgia had been executing on a strategic business plan to convert the foundation of her business from essentially a boutique, transaction-based business to a sustainable and predictable book of business. To do this, she had to establish a new ideal customer profile and focus on improving the size and buying power of this targeted set of ideal customers. This proved to be tougher than she anticipated. In essence, Georgia had to *fire* the low profit customers (lower margins, no-win bids, lower size orders, no predictability, and high maintenance–clients that produced a low ROR). These customers had to be replaced with new relationships that would not only give her preferred status for purchasing, but would utilize her talents to help them with strategic initiatives (which typically have a plan, budget and long-term predictability to them).

The second year into her plan, and due to the downturn in the economy, the volume of annual business and income Georgia traditionally placed had fallen off substantially. Some of this was of her choosing and some not. Management was nervous and concerned—the pressure on all sides was pretty strong. Sticking to the long-term plan was extremely difficult.

But Georgia did not go back to taking whatever came in to make a buck, nor did she succumb to a reactionary style that often accompanies sales slumps and the fear factor that comes with them. During times of stress we tend to drop everything to be busy or to turn the order—when the completion of very specific strategic activities for building and growing our business are just as essential (if not immediately visible in result).

The first cornerstone of success in her new approach came through cultivating a Champion in a long-term client she had retained because of the strategic potential. She successfully nurtured this one relationship and moved *up the ladder* to eventually implement a nation-wide program connecting buyers for her products across the nation. She rolled out a uniquely customized portfolio of additional services that awarded her preferred status and put specific programs in place for leveraging the company's *go-to-marketing* initiatives. Working with this very creative and high-energy Champion, she also leveraged her experience in that industry to target and eventually land other additional clients that mirrored this client profile.

A further exciting outcome is that this Champion accepted a new job with greater responsibility and invited Georgia to become part of his strategic plans at his new company. She continues to collaborate with Mike in very strategic approaches to growing revenue for each of his business divisions of the company.

She didn't stop there. Having established her ideal target profile, she targeted several other companies with whom she had never done business. She leveraged referrals, a consistent outreach process and marketing and sales tactics over a full year prior to seeing a substantial turn in response to her efforts.

Now, in addition to a better set of traditional accounts (mostly managed by her team), she has four cornerstone accounts for which she has indeed become a Value Creator. They definitely would ALL say, *"I don't know what the company did **BEFORE** you."*

And since it is such a great story, I'll add a little more detail here on one of the clients who took close to a year to get in front of. Eventually (frankly by being persistent and clever) she landed a meeting with the person she perceived to be the potential Champion. She interviewed Eric, found out what he valued, what his pain points with his current program were and what his vision was for expanding his personal influence in the company. Ironically, Eric was attempting to treat his current vendor as a Value Creator—but that service provider kept acting like just a vendor—offering only to take orders and provide minimal services. The incumbent was doing very little—if anything—to help impact process and service improvements for Eric.

Georgia got to understand the values and motivators for Eric, the challenges for implementing strategies he had in mind and what Eric wanted and needed from a business partner who could deliver the products needed to accomplish these goals.

Ask Yourself

⇒ How many of your clients are verified Champions?

⇒ How many of these Champions know you as a Value Creator?

Value Creators keep on creating new value for their clients. Everybody keeps on winning.

By understanding the goals for Eric's programs, Georgia was able to collaborate on and design a program that replaced a multi-million dollar legacy program completely with a solution that in year one would save over $200,000 in product liability alone for the customer. This program required a blend of new roles for people, another powerful business partner, better and more efficient processes, and industry technologies more suited to the client's needs.

Six months after the launch of the program, we pulled together extensive analysis and YOY expenditures to provide a comprehensive report for the management team. The goal was to showcase the value Georgia and the other partner, Chas, had created for the client; but MOST important was the intent to arm Eric with information so that he could articulate tangible results and achievements made over the first six months. This is what a value creator does – they coach and consult with their client and co-workers to create and report on results. This team pulled together the materials for a major presentation to the executive management team. This meeting set the direction for leveraging the infrastructure and reporting data of the program to allow management to make informed business decisions with regard to this product category for the company. Another result of the process is that Eric is establishing himself as a value creator for his company.

For her business overall, Georgia went from being a preferred vendor for hundreds of customers to having a portfolio of profitable and rewarding clients. Now her time is spent in being a Value Creator for a select few clients and her fantastic team operates to support these traditional clients. As a result, she has exceeded prior sales years in year three of the plan. Further, Georgia is now positioned to grow from here with a business model to scale sales and the support team. This team has been developed and mentored to reflect her principles as a Value Creator to all clients—regardless of the relationships or selling status. Together, Georgia and her team are irreplaceable to these clients, strategically integrated into their Champion's goals and a vital part of many people's lives.

Value Creator—Defining Characteristics

1. **Continuous Learning:** Become an expert in your target clients' industry verticals.
2. **Self-Management:** Create work environment to support proactive and strategic focus on clients.
3. **Planning:** Know the life-time value of client relationships and work a 3 year plan.
4. **Sales and Marketing:** Refine leadership skills in community and industry.

	Rank each statement on a scale of 1 to 10. 1 is limited competence. 10 is highly competent.	Rank
Learn	• I continue to do research on the best practices, technology and networking resources to grow myself professionally and personally. • I discover additional methods to help reveal and release my untapped potential and better utilize the tools and resources I already have access to. I continually source new tools and resources. • I attend advanced sales or business webinars or events to uncover and explore new pathways for creating value across my customer base. • I focus on what is important to my client and try to understand their motivations and challenges from their perspective. They view me as the expert.	
Think	• I look for ways to improve the quality of my service by thinking like a client. What do they expect from a world class firm? How can I meet and exceed their expectations? • I consider how I can become the *trusted advisor* to clients. How do my actions and systems support that objective? • I ask myself what my clients perceive as value. I continually think about what can be improved and I actively engage clients in providing feedback on the quality of my services.	
Act	• I have written a 3 year strategic plan for my business to include long-term goals that I break down into actionable monthly goals. • I focus on building my business and I measure everything. I know my numbers and track all activities measured against business growth goals and strategies. • I regularly review and refine my operations manual on team process directives for the business. I have systems for everything so anyone can operate the administrative side of my business. • I have invested in personnel to help with the daily operation, transaction management and administration of the business. This allows me time to focus on client relationships and client acquisition activities. • I am continually inventing new ways to talk to my customers and introduce ideas they may have not considered as part of providing an *out of the box* thinking to them	
Accelerate	• I stay focused on creating an experience of excellence for clients. They know what I stand for and how I am serving in a role that will benefit them personally and professionally. • I place all energy and attention on helping clients get the answers to their biggest challenges. My expertise and services assure them. This is value creation of the highest order. • I take a courageous stand on helping clients reclaim their vision for their contribution to their company. I commit and dedicate myself to that purpose to establish and build my business.	

Ask Yourself

Review these questions to clarify, for yourself, how you compare to a top producer. Consider how a top producer might answer these questions. Then what is the reality for yourself?

Continuous Learning	• What is your plan for learning how to build your business beyond a personal practice? What resources do you draw upon for expanding your business knowledge of your target customer profile? • What is your understanding of your ability to create value for your clients beyond the sale of product solutions or programs? What do you read and study to improve your knowledge and personal value?
Self-Management	• How do you develop leadership capabilities and how do you demonstrate your understanding of your leadership role in providing exemplary service to your clients? • What are your plans for creating a professional Master Mind Group? How will this help you to advance your business goals and provide additional value for your clients?
Planning	• What needs to happen to become both strategically important and hard to replace with the customers and prospects that meet your ideal customer profile? • What systems have you created and implemented that continue to provide you with a steady stream of highly qualified prospects? What is your formal plan for improving results? • What is your plan for maintaining a level of current clients that you can effectively service? How will you reduce the service load of having too many clients?
Sales and Marketing Skills	• How can you improve your marketing and outreach communications to showcase your value beyond simple product delivery to clients? What is the key activity that provides consistent results in client acquisition? • How do you communicate the value of your expertise and then conduct marketing campaigns that leverage that expertise? How do you describe your referral process? How effective is it in obtaining introductions to highly qualified prospects? • Do you have a *Dream Team* of prospects that you would love to have in your portfolio? What research or study are you doing to understand how to replace the competition and become integrated into the clients' strategic initiatives?

Your Notes

Crossing the Gap Action Planner—Beyond Value Creator

1. Create Your Gap List

Consider the Defining Characteristics listed on page 131. Which characteristics do you need to improve in order to move yourself toward the Preferred Status quadrant? Write your answers here or in your journal for each gap identified. Start with no more than three gaps. Once you complete your initial gaps, you can work on others. Copy of this page permitted.

GAP: (write your specific gap here)	ANSWERS
What do you need to learn to help you cross this gap?	
How do you need to think differently about this gap or situation? Who might give you a different perspective to consider?	
How will what you learn change your mindset and accelerate you toward your objective?	
What are the types of actions you plan to take?	

2. Action Plan

What specific actions do you plan to take?

Based on the gaps identified in *Learn, Think, Act, Accelerate* on page 131, what is one or more actions you plan to take to improve your situation and help you master this quadrant?

- How will these actions make you *Strategically Important* and Hard to *Replace*?
- How will these actions increase your understanding of your clients' situations and business needs?
- How will you know you have mastered this quadrant?

My Planned Actions	Start Date	Complete Date

PART FOUR

THE (Z) FACTOR

ZFACTOR BUTTERFLY EFFECT

CAPABILITIES

CAPACITY FOR CHANGE

Part Four

The ZFactor Butterfly Effect

Right Thoughts and Right Actions Create Momentum

Throughout this book you have been called to think and act differently about yourself, your clients and your business. Hopefully you are becoming confident in the benefits received from changing your mindset and ways of doing business. This requires coming from the center of all that is going on, in and around you, and having an outward focus on the successful business and life you desire. It's about making a difference in the lives of others.

The Butterfly Effect describes the phenomenon where one small change or event at one place in time can result in large changes happening at a later date in time. The butterfly effect has been a common storyline in time-travel movies, where the key character goes back in time and in changing even the smallest of things drastically impacts different experiences in years to come, often with a vast results. The *Back to the Future* movies demonstrate the butterfly effect. To provide a more realistic example, let's say you create an unexpected value for a client. That client tells someone else what you did for them and the value it gave them. This sets off a chain of events—and the result could be one day you receive a request from a new prospect (most often happening through email or social network introduction these days) who becomes a new client.

People who empower the butterfly effect have moved from participating in groups such as networking organizations where the question is *"What's in it for me?"* to serving in capacities as volunteers, on non-profit boards, churches, schools, Rotary Club, Chamber of Commerce or other service-focused organizations where the focus is *"What's in it for others?"* They often take informal leadership or mentor roles within their companies and community and expect no compensation or recognition in return. It becomes a sense of duty or a calling to give back to others, be a part of making a difference and live a life of significance with meaning and purpose.

A seemingly irrelevant event on the other side of the planet can have a direct impact on the daily life of a sales professional.

Apply the defining characteristics of the Value Creator and experience the law of momentum in your business.

We now live in times when it often feels like an insignificant event or change on the other side of the planet can have a direct impact on our daily life. WWTED (What will the Euro do)? Who will be President? Why did the IPO of that company not perform as planned? What new device will cause another to be obsolete? How will China impact our product pricing strategy? While there is no way to control such happenings, we have to consider a paradigm of thinking for learning and understanding how to manage various risks as it relates to change, uncertainties and the unknown.

Just as any event outside of your control can seem to work against you, so can you empower the butterfly effect to work for you. Every action we take and interaction we engage in has consequences. It is the integrity brought to each moment and the mind-wrestling experienced when evaluating opportunity vs. risk that our character as Value Creators is shaped and molded. We will never know when a *no* given today (either *to* you or *by* you) will turn back around in our favor… either way the ripples of decisions and associated responses and results live on.

The Butterfly effect begins with the *affect* that the Value Creator has on the surrounding world simply because the values, beliefs and standards are interwoven into all they are and do. This doesn't mean one can avoid dealing with conflict. In these days and times it is nearly impossible to be highly competitive without having values and standards challenged at some time or another. However, when grounded in integrity and knowledge of who you are, even those conflicts will eventually pan out to support positive outcomes in the future. True life-long comrades on the path to Value Creator show up in very unexpected ways (com·rade *noun* a person who shares in one's activities, occupation, etc.; companion, associate, or friend)!

But what is the true impact of doing or *not* doing? While it is natural to focus on the stuff happening to *you*, keep in mind unexpected things happen to your clients, as well. Your role is to create value and be there when clients weather times of change or challenging and difficult times. Mastering the ability to think and act differently becomes a beneficial hedge during times of change and uncertainty. It becomes the guiding influence for what we choose to do or not. The greater the capacity for dealing with both will bring more value to clients, which, in turn, will increase sales and business growth.

When you consistently do the right stuff, and remain disciplined in planning, the resulting actions will build momentum for your business.

Make the ZFactor Butterfly Effect Work for You

As you have progressed through ZFactor, you have been encouraged to reflect on what it takes to be strategically important and hard to replace with your clients. Hopefully, you have practiced this continually and converted your new thinking ability into a habit for personal and professional development for accelerating sales performance.

Now, let's put all of this together. Consider the Three Key Factors below as a recipe to manage the day-to-day risks of change, uncertainty, chaos and the unknown.

1. **Know Yourself:**

   ⇒ Be a continuous learner about who you are, your strengths, weaknesses, skills, abilities, competencies, knowledge, and experiences.

   ⇒ Read good books and associate with other learners who think about much different things than you.

   ⇒ Find a mentor and a coach who will challenge you to always be accountable to the best you can be.

   ⇒ Take various assessments, gain insight into how you think and act, and most importantly, reflect often on how you react or respond to situations around that involve change and uncertainty.

2. **Know Your Clients:**

   ⇒ Always be curious about other people.

   ⇒ Get to know details about your clients.

   ⇒ Be more interested in getting to know them than trying to get them interested in you.

   ⇒ Be willing to take risks and know you will be disappointed in other people, at times. Even so, continue to be curious and a student of human behavior.

   ⇒ Practice your listening, observation and presentation skills. Get coaching on becoming a better listener, observer and presenter.

"It is one of the beautiful compensations of this life that no man can sincerely try to help another without helping himself... Serve and thou shall be served."

~ Ralph Waldo Emerson ~

Sales Accelerator

The size of the intersection in the three circles reveals the potential you have to create value for your clients.

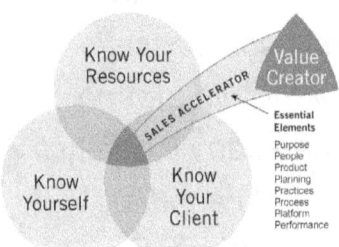

3. **Know Your Resources:**

⇒ Resources are tangible tools, systems, and people that you have access to and can leverage to make something happen.

⇒ Resources can be people, books, technology, marketing materials, product information, industry data, white papers, software, applications and equipment.

⇒ With experience, participation in an accountability group, and continual study and engagement in training opportunities you can learn when to apply specific resources to create the right solutions for your clients.

Knowing yourself, your clients and your resources, and where these three key factors intersect, will reveal the potential you have for creating value for your clients. Most successful people who are Value Creators learn this over a long period of time and through much experience. With a little understanding and intention, you can achieve this ability to be a Value Creator much faster. This intersection point is called the *Value Creator Intersection*.

As you fully embrace the defining characteristics of the Value Creator, you will experience the law of momentum in your business. Consistently create value for others and your sales will grow. Invest time and money in yourself and your business to become the best you can be and continue to get better at all you do. The result will be a successful and sustainable business.

Take time to review and reflect on the *PROACT Action Plan to Increase Revenue and Income* for the ZFactor Butterfly Effect. If you have more work to do to complete the exercise to *Cross Your Success Gap*, keep in mind the *Three Key Factors* and how the actions you take will enlarge the area where the three factors intersect.

The better you have identified and clarified each *Essential Element* for yourself and your business the greater your sales acceleration.

Ask Yourself

⇒ Where have you seen the butterfly effect at work in your life?

⇒ Where is there activity or momentum occurring that you could tap into and leverage?

⇒ Which of your clients are creating a ripple effect in their personal or professional lives and what are you doing to develop your relationship with them?

⇒ What resources are available to you to help you reach a wider audience?

⇒ How can you leverage your networking and social networking to put the power of the ZFactor Butterfly Effect at work for you?

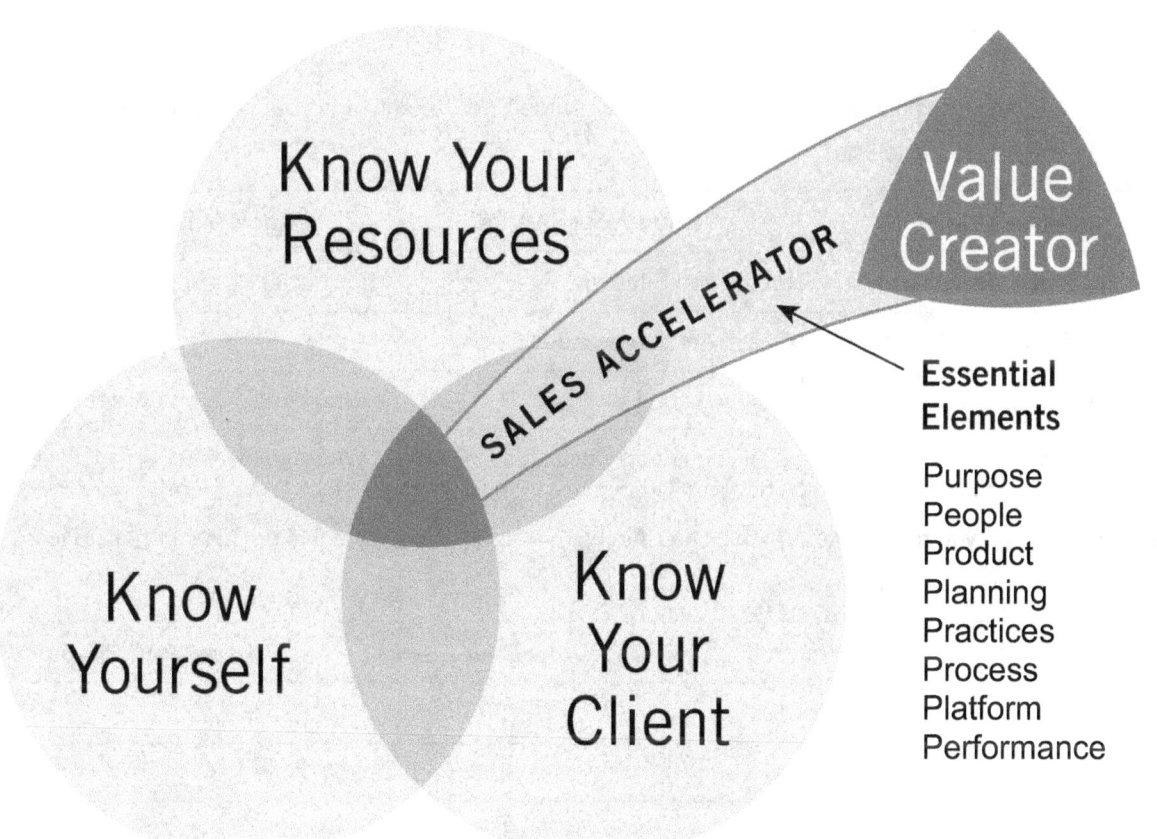

Empower the ZFactor Butterfly Effect to Make You a Value Creator

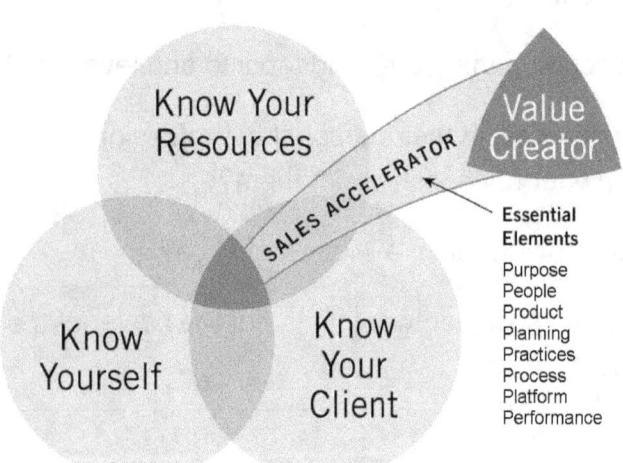

Essential
Elements

Purpose
People
Product
Planning
Practices
Process
Platform
Performance

Embrace your unique role as a catalyst and partner for your clients' business success. Your desires to live and work with a sense of purpose and meaning will drive you to know more about yourself, your clients and your resources. As you achieve higher levels of success by serving more and more clients, we encourage you to celebrate the impact you have on others.

This is a list of items for you to consider to better know yourself, your clients and your resources. What other items might you add to these lists?

Know Yourself	Know Your Clients	Know Your Resources
Strengths, Skills and Weaknesses	Profile and Situation	Products, People and Processes
Goals, Ambitions and Objectives	Goals, Ambitions and Objectives	Tools and Techniques
Priorities and Plans	Priorities and Plans	Who and Where to Access
Presentation Method	Challenges and Obstacles	Where to Invest

What are the things you need to Learn, Think and Act upon that will Accelerate this process for getting to know yourself, your clients and your resources?

Questions	Know Yourself	Know Your Clients	Know Your Resources
Learn			
Think			
Act			
Accelerate			

PART FIVE

THE (Z) FACTOR

CONCLUDING THOUGHTS

Chapter 5
Concluding Thoughts

What's Next? Become a Value Creator

Fast forward a few months. Just like Pat, you have completed the work in the book, you have a plan of action and you are consistently executing your plan and achieving your objectives. During these past few months, you have most likely experienced numerous limiting mindsets that made you realize what has held you back from achieving your goals.

You are now in possession of the knowledge, tools, and method by which you may accelerate your sales performance. You hold in your hands the keys to unlock the door that will enable you to reach the Pinnacle of success. The question remains, what will you choose to do? Will you summon the courage to attain your full potential and to become a Value Creator - one who is Strategically Important and Hard to replace?

Now, is the time to put your foot to the accelerator to close the gap between where you are now and where you want to be with your career.

Concluding Thoughts and the 30 day Challenge

In Lewis Carroll's book, Alice In Wonderland, the King says, *"Begin at the beginning, and go on til you come to the end: then stop."* That is where we are in this book. We have had a grand start, an adventuresome journey, and now we have come to the end. It is time to stop. However, there is room for one more quote, this from Thomas Henry Huxley. *"The great end of life is not knowledge, but action."*

We heard you say, "Now what?" What comes next is a simple plan that you can operate on a daily basis. It requires only your attention, focus, and commitment. We challenge you to engage fully in the process for at least 30-days, knowing that if you do this, it will become a habit and your ultimate

It's time to put your foot to the accelerator and close the gap between where you are and where you want to be.

"What lies behind us and what lies before us are tiny matters compared to what lies within us."

~ Ralph Waldo Emerson ~

success is assured. Remember, you are the one to decide what success means to you. Whatever it is, define it and write it down. Follow the proven formula of having a major definite purpose, a definite plan to achieve that purpose, and a plan of action to accomplish the fulfillment of your purpose. With that as the set up, let's move on to the 30-day challenge.

Next, examine your results every 30-days. What were your average sales results at the start and what are you seeing at the end of the 30-day period? How does it feel to be more focused, more accountable, more productive, and more successful?

The intent of this book is to provide a map and a simple set of instructions for how to accelerate your journey to the pinnacle of success. Yes, the content was about knowledge but there was something more—a call to action! Go back through the book and look at the exercises and Ask Yourself questions. You did build an action plan, didn't you? Remember Huxley's words about the great end of life? He was saying that knowledge is good but action is the purpose of life.

Successful people think differently and take action once they know what to do and how to do it. We also know that thinking differently and knowledge alone will not amount to much of a change. Action is the catalyst, and the will to act comes from internal motivation. Internal motivation is driven by one's values and the emotions attached to those values. It is also clear that success is the result of who you are being and not just based on what you do. Your desire to advance relationships from being just a vendor to being a Value Creator is noble. The Value Creator contributes so much value for the benefit of their client that they become *Strategically Important* and *Hard to Replace*. How much of a difference do you want to make for your clients?

Determine where you are, decide where you want to be, get out your ZMap, and plot your course of action. The gap between the two points is your untapped potential. On a real road trip, you check your car, check your supplies, and pack your bags. Same here, check your thinking, check your knowledge and skills, and pack your briefcase. Build out your Action Plan and hit the road! It is doable and you are unstoppable, if you choose to be.

The choice is yours. Carpe Diem!

THE NEXT STORY BEGINS… and it's YOURS!

> You now have the tools and knowledge to accelerate your sales performance. It is only a matter of execution by you.

APPENDIX

THE Ⓩ FACTOR

ZMAP EXAMPLES—BUILD YOUR OWN

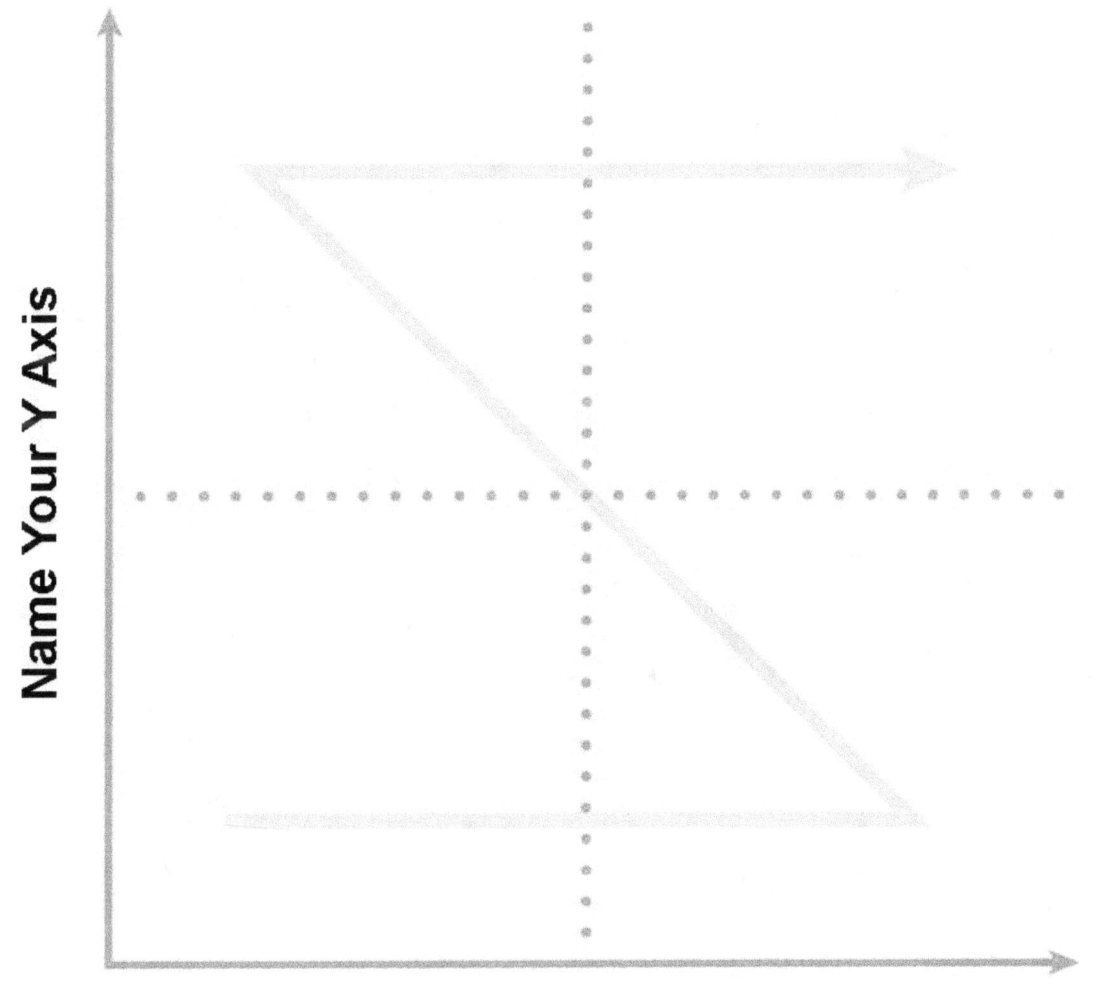

Name Your Y Axis

Name Your X Axis

The Thinking Framework™

Choose What You Want to Think

Reveal and Release Untapped Potential

Written by Alan W. Goldsberry, Creator of the Thinking Framework™

Skillful thinking is essential for improving performance. The Thinking Framework has been intentionally designed to assist an individual to develop the skill for thinking and acting differently. The Thinking Framework utilizes a proprietary coaching methodology that activates a focused process to equip an individual to clearly observe, identify, analyze and evaluate current performance challenges in order to reveal specific actions to release untapped potential for success.

This methodology utilizes a customized *XY* graph, called a ZMap, as a visual aid to rapidly identify essential elements for successful actions, characteristics, skills, resources, values, attitudes and behaviors. The Thinking Framework makes it easier for an individual to gain clarity and quickly accelerate their success as they adapt and implement various elements to fit who they are and where they are. Equipped with this information, one's level of achievement is based solely upon their level of willing engagement, persistence and desire to succeed.

When the Thinking Framework is combined with the ZFactor coaching methodology, this establishes a solid foundation for accelerating success for those In the product sales profession.

How ZMaps are Designed to Focus on the Right Stuff

A well designed ZMap helps an individual to rapidly focus on essential elements that make a difference. A ZMap opens with a question designed to address a challenge or other situation. For example the question, "What makes you strategically important and hard to replace with your clients?"

Hard to Replace identifies the *X* axis and *Strategically Important* identifies the *Y* axis for the starting ZMap presented in this book Then key

Rapid acceleration toward achievement or your goals.

concepts and essential elements of success are organized into a learning and development process within the *XY* graph. Based upon one's knowledge, attitude, resources, experiences and skills, an individual can easily plot *where they are* in the learning and development process. This allows them to focus on what they need, at that time.

Traditional training, learning and development requires an individual to review and take in a lot of different information and data before they can focus on the right information that fits them and what they need. It is a difficult process to find a solution that works for every individual, given their unique characteristics and capabilities. Training is designed to download data and information to an individual who then, on their own, must figure out what works or does not work for them.

As to the coaching process, many professional coaches do not have direct experience and success in the specific profession of the individual they are coaching. While the coach may be highly skilled in the art and craft of coaching, they may not have the experience of knowing what it really takes to be successful in their clients' line of sales. They ask probing questions to activate an individual's thinking, but the individual is left to roam around in their own thoughts and ideas. So the individual is left with trying to determine what specific characteristics for success they must identify and create a plan for. The individual only knows what they know and the coach cannot provide experienced advice.

When an individual seeks to improve performance they need a blend of training, information gathering, advice and coaching in order to fully integrate new ideas, skills and behaviors into daily practices. The best coaches are those who have specific experience and success in the profession. This is why an organization will experience a high ROI when they train and coach sales managers to develop coaching skills.

Why ZFactor Works

A well constructed ZMap establishes a visual aid that provides a simple and proven pathway of essential elements toward success. We call this *"Meeting You Where You Are."* The moment an individual knows where they are, the natural instinct is to identify where they want to go. The ZFactor

> The best sales coaches have developed coaching skills with peer experience and proven success that meet or exceed your ambitions.

process assists the individual to cross this gap by assimilating the defining characteristics of Top Producers into their everyday work-life.

ZFactor works because it has fully integrated the best of the best. The ZFactor methodology uncovers the defining characteristics of Top Producers, which have been tested and proven to create results. These characteristics are distilled into essential elements of success and then organized into a pathway of learning and development. Now an individual can quickly and easily assess where they are along the pathway and focus on what they need now to improve their performance.

Many sales management and sales trainings today pop out canned sales tips or techniques without knowing anything about the sales professional's unique starting place needs, skills and experience. The best sales managers, trainers and coaches embrace the full learning and development process beginning with an assessment in order to focus on the unique needs of the professional. This is why the ZFactor coaching method is a perfect companion to popular and effective sales training systems. Then managers can coach or mentor the professional through the process of mastering new skills and behaviors while utilizing their strengths and resources to move them along the pathway to success.

No matter where an individual starts on this pathway, they can acknowledge and identify specific actions to take to improve their performance. They can quickly assess themselves within the ZMap based upon essential ingredients that are proven to drive success. By simply ranking themselves to best practices and characteristics of success an individual can identify specific gaps and then put together a simple action plan to bridge the gap toward achievement. This is why the ZFactor methodology works.

ZFactor works when you are inspired and motivated to make changes to improve your performance.

The Key Ingredients of the Thinking Framework—Build a One Page Book

- **View # 1:** Measures ability to master the relationship skills and/or behaviors required to adopt the defining characteristics. As one embraces and engages into mastering all the characteristics, they progress across the X axis.

- **View # 2:** Measures level of performance as it relates to a specific activity within an area or profession. As an individual adapts and integrates defining characteristics of success, they will progress up the Y axis.

- **The Quadrants:** Identifies the pathway of success with key concepts, practices, processes and ideas (the Defining Characteristics). They describe the personal and/or professional development necessary to achieve better performance results and to progress to the next quadrant.

- **The Backward Z:** The titles and details within the quadrants summarize the process. This makes it easy for someone to quickly know where they are and what they have to do to get to where they want to be.

Execute

- Build a strategy of the practices and processes you developed with the intention to establish better practices.

- Planning becomes essential for creating consistent and sustainable success.

- Develop plan and process for creating lifetime value of opportunity.

Evaluate & Innovate

- Ongoing evaluation of new results based upon changes.

- Make appropriate adjustments and create new ideas and strategies.

- Be a Value Creator.

Acknowledge & Identify

- Acknowledge performance requirements for results and identify challenges.

- Identify specific actions, practices, disciplines, processes and behaviors that will improve performance.

- Determine if your thoughts and actions are more reactionary or responsive.

Development

- Ask thought provoking questions to clarify skills, values, knowledge, experience and available resources (people, process, tools).

- Make initial changes. Use To Do, Stop Do and 'Who Do' lists.

- Design a process uniquely customized to your needs. Observe changes in speech, attitudes, behaviors and actions.

VIEW # 2 (vertical axis label)

VIEW # 1 (horizontal axis label)

Example: ZMap Overview—Sales Growth ZMap

ZMaps are like one page books. A well constructed ZMap contains all the primary concepts of a situation with the flexibility for the user to customize the ZMap to fit their personal situation. ZMaps help one to hold two complimentary or contradictory thoughts at the same time. This will stimulate new thinking and make it easy for one to review and track progress. This is the Sales Growth ZMap Terry shows to Pat to start him thinking differently about his situation. When Pat first looked at the Sales Growth ZMap, he plotted himself in the **Preferred Status** quadrant. He came to this conclusion when he realized he had not mastered the sales process, as of yet. He was also curious about the Value Creator quadrant.

- What were you first thoughts about the Sales Growth ZMap?

- How have those thoughts changed after learning more about ZFactor and the ZMaps?

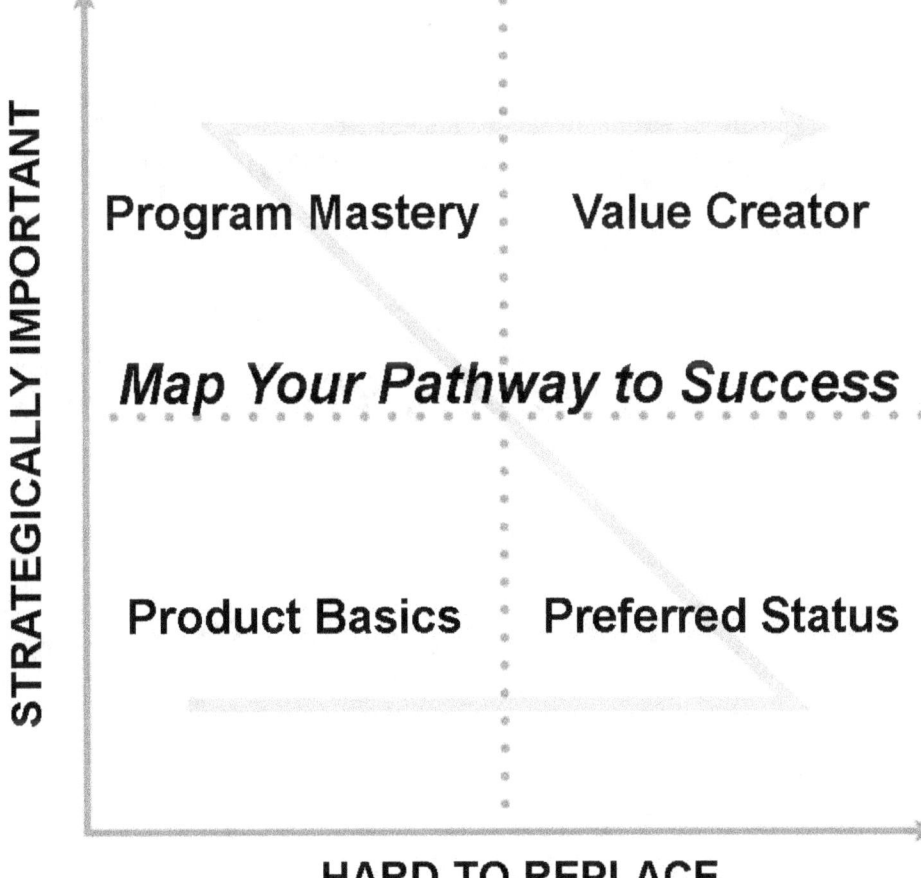

See the other ZMaps on the following pages...

Example: Skill Development ZMap

The *Skill Development ZMap* demonstrates the impact of this principle. As you improve your skills and competencies, you increase your value to others. As you increase your personal and professional value to others, they begin to see you as a *Value Creator*. This process requires that Warrior Spirit because you have to be willing to make the necessary changes to achieve success.

- What changes have you made in your thoughts and actions?

- How are these changes motivating or inspiring you to become a top producer?

Example: Accomplishment ZMap—College

The *Accomplishment ZMap* demonstrates the correlation between discipline and accomplishment. The better one exercises focused disciplines the greater their accomplishments. This ZMap was used by Terry's wife to help their son realize the value of being disciplined about his schoolwork and other school activities, such as establishing good study habit and keeping those throughout his high school and college career. This simple correlation gave him the understanding to envision how his goals of a specific college were achievable if he just did the basics. With the basics his natural talents and abilities were able to shine.

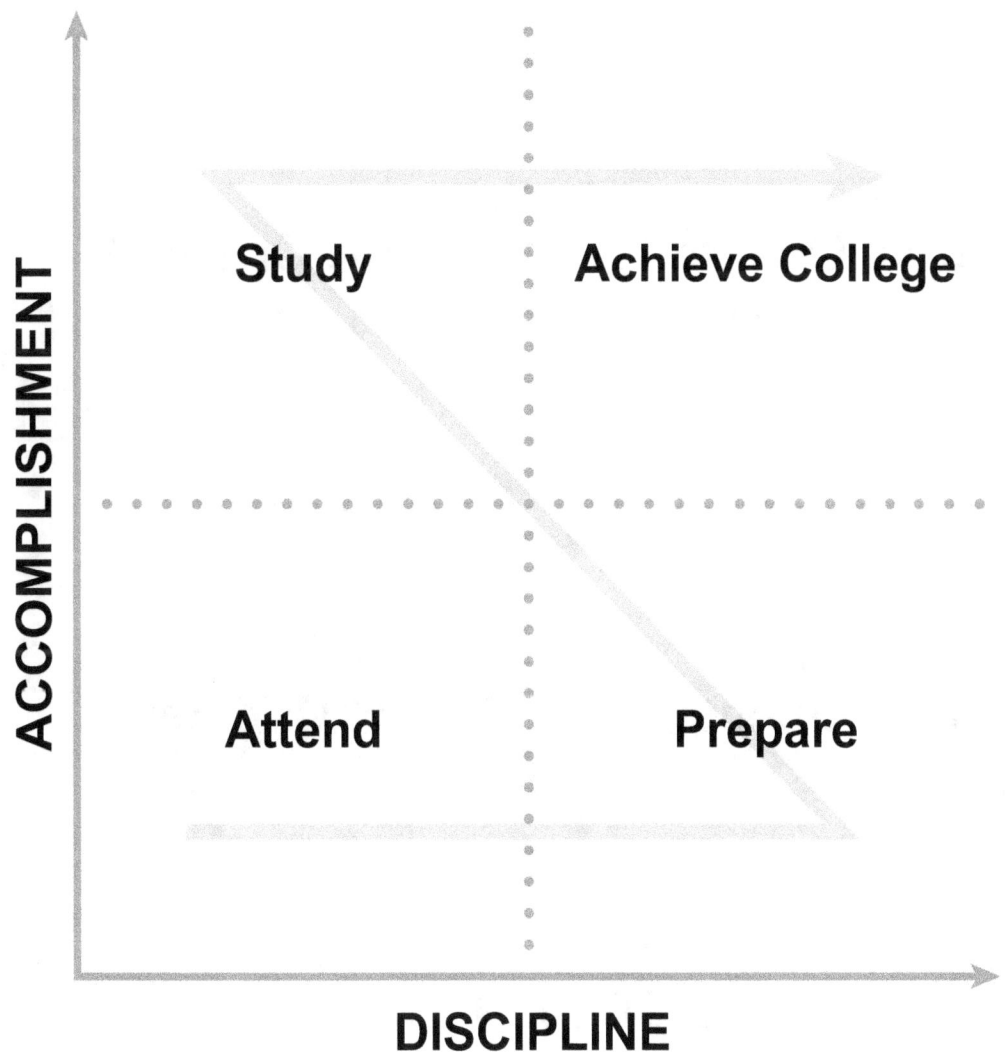

Example: Accomplishment ZMap—Business

The *Accomplishment ZMap* demonstrates the correlation between discipline and accomplishment. The better one exercises focused disciplines the greater their accomplishments. Consider which orientation most represents your strengths. Then consider who can you trust or depend upon to take care of the other styles.

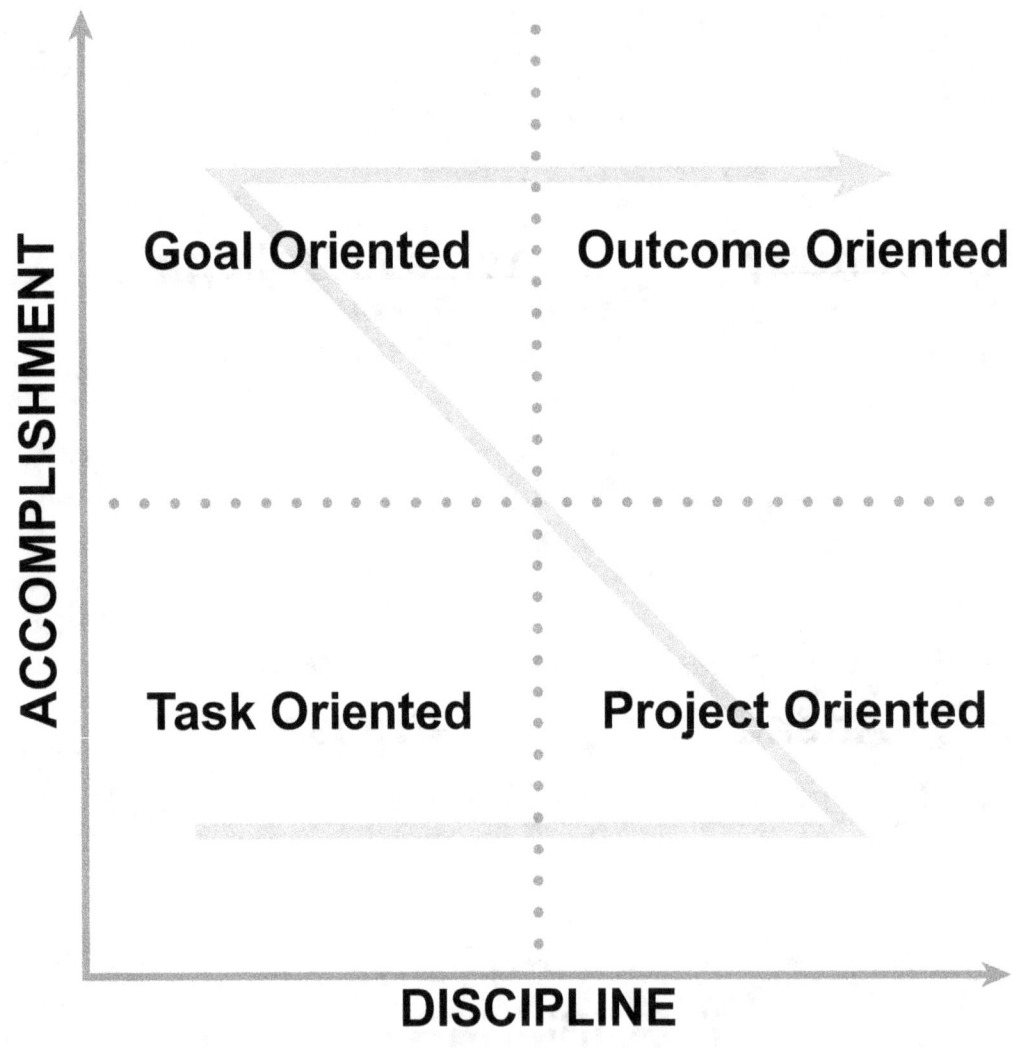

Example: Your Personal ZMap

Plot your progression on your personal ZMap. How will you customize the ZMap to fit you and your situation? Fill in each quadrant like Pat did. See his example on the next page.

Note: For each quadrant write goals for:
- ⇒ Continuous Learning
- ⇒ Self Management
- ⇒ Planning
- ⇒ Sales and Marketing

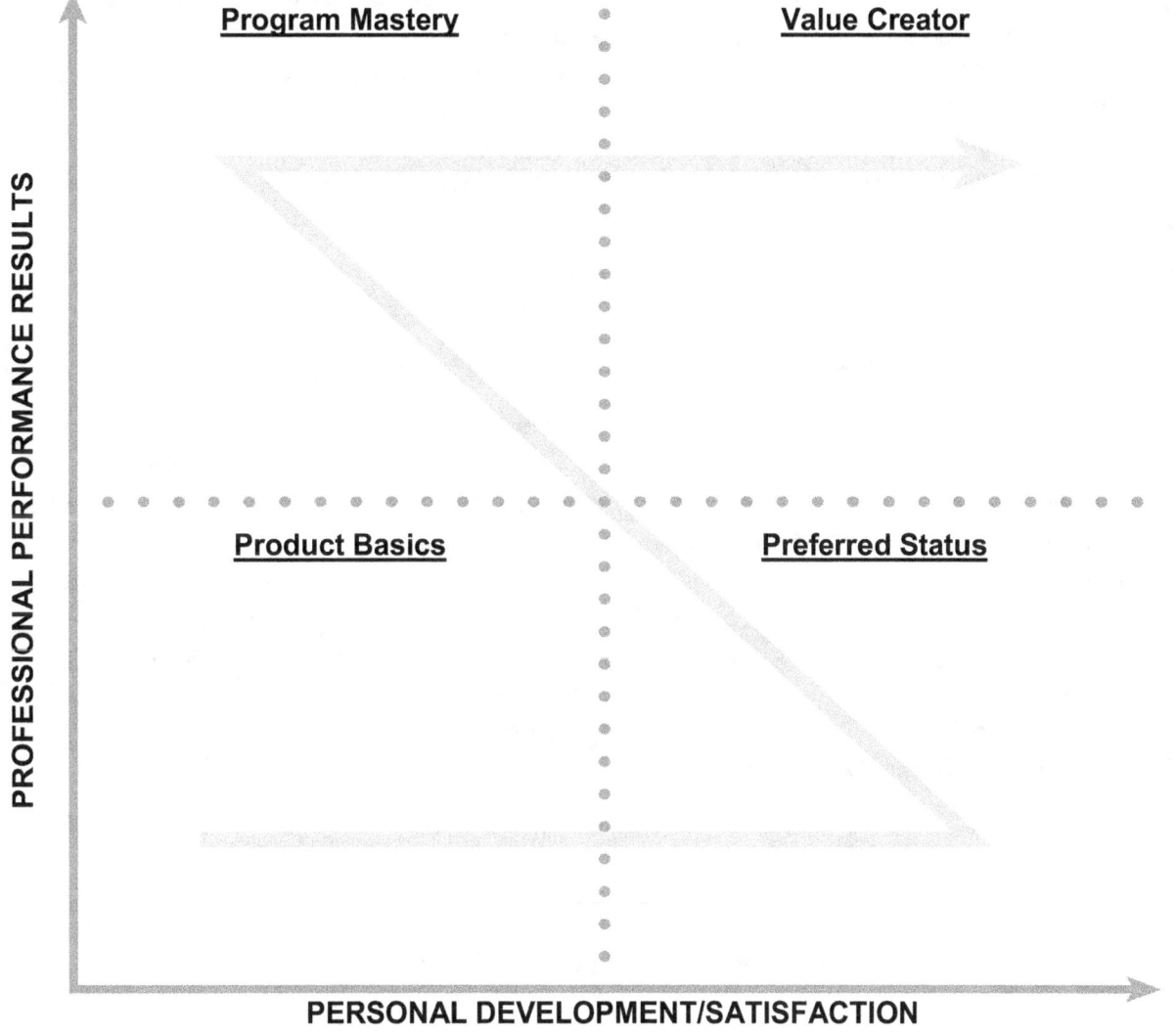

PROFESSIONAL PERFORMANCE RESULTS

Program Mastery

Value Creator

Product Basics

Preferred Status

PERSONAL DEVELOPMENT/SATISFACTION

Example: Pat's Personal ZMap

Program Mastery

- **Continuous Learning**
  - Learn more about what procurement professionals value.
- **Self-Management**
  - Find a professional organization and volunteer.
- **Planning**
  - Learn more about the kind of processes I can offer to clients.
- **Sales and Marketing**
  - As I build my sales system, write it out so I eventually have a step by step process.

Value Creator

- **Continuous Learning**
  - Start getting more familiar with industry verticals.
- **Self-Management**
  - Use my volunteer activities to begin developing my leadership skills.
  - Start up a peer book study group. Use ZFactor.
- **Planning**
  - Write my 1 year plan. Make planning a daily routine, so I can learn faster.
- **Sales and Marketing**
  - Interview my top 3 clients and ask them how I can (or do) create value for them.

Product Basics

- **Continuous Learning**
  - Get competent in two new products.
- **Self-Management**
  - Only do things during the day that make money.
- **Planning**
  - Have at least a simple 'To Do' and 'Stop Do' list
  - Set my activity goals and track them at the end of each day.
- **Sales and Marketing**
  - Get an initial client profile completed.

Preferred Status

- **Continuous Learning**
  - Read the sales book Terry referred to me.
  - Join a Toastmasters to improve my presentation skills.
- **Self-Management**
  - Develop a list of specific questions to ask clients to help them gain more value when meeting with me.
  - Block time for relationship client prospecting.
- **Planning**
  - Update my CRM program and organize my activities and office to support my sales activities.
- **Sales and Marketing**
  - Write out all my sales processes.
  - Use my client profile to request referrals.

SALES PERFORMANCE

PERSONAL & PROFESSIONAL DEVELOPMENT

Example: Thinking Framework™
Reveal and Release Untapped Potential

ACTION

Strategic Change

- Strategic thinking skills are developed to manage relationships and resources.
- Integrating new ideas and concepts into daily practices and life.
- Desires and embraces change.
- Building significant capacity for managing change and dealing with the unknown.
- Changes personal thoughts, at will, yet maintains strong personal/professional values.
- Self-value realized and released.
- Explores new conversations with others.
- Clear vision, mission, goals. Service minded.
- People are attracted to you.
- Work takes on meaning and purpose.

Transformation

- Systems thinking skills are critical to leverage and synergize all available resources for growth.
- Living a meaningful, purpose-driven life.
- Influential. Others seek you out because of your focus on making a difference.
- Mentoring and leading others. Self-fulfilled.
- One of success to significance.
- Deep understanding for how to manage Thought + Action = Result.
- Highly skilled at managing chaos, change and dealing with the unknown.
- Work is integrated into your purpose-driven life.

RESULTS

Exploring Change

- Becoming aware of specific mindsets that no longer support new goals or ambitions.
- Fear of the future becomes a motivation to seek information to understand the risks.
- Learning to replace automatic reactions with thoughtful responses.
- Seek out trusted sources for people who have successfully replaced similar mindsets.
- Integration Both/And thinking into all basic attitudes and daily practices.
- Become better informed, thinking through various situations and responses increases confidence to overcome old behavioral responses and mindsets.

Managing Change

- Both/And thinking becomes a key habit making persistence a discipline.
- Strengthen personal/professional values.
- Self-focused and self-interested for self improvement purposes, not for selfish gain.
- Observing, being curious, responsive behaviors.
- Values all relationships by actively listening.
- Evolving and expecting the best. Work takes on a new meaning. Growth potential realized and pursued.
- Question old mindsets. Irrelevant thoughts are released.
- Focus on how you want to be perceived.
- Growing awareness and understanding of surroundings and personal impact on such.

THOUGHT

Business Builder ZMaps

The following ZMaps are various ZMaps that have been used in situations to help people grow their business. These "one page books" are used to help people think about and stay focused on the right stuff to grow their business.

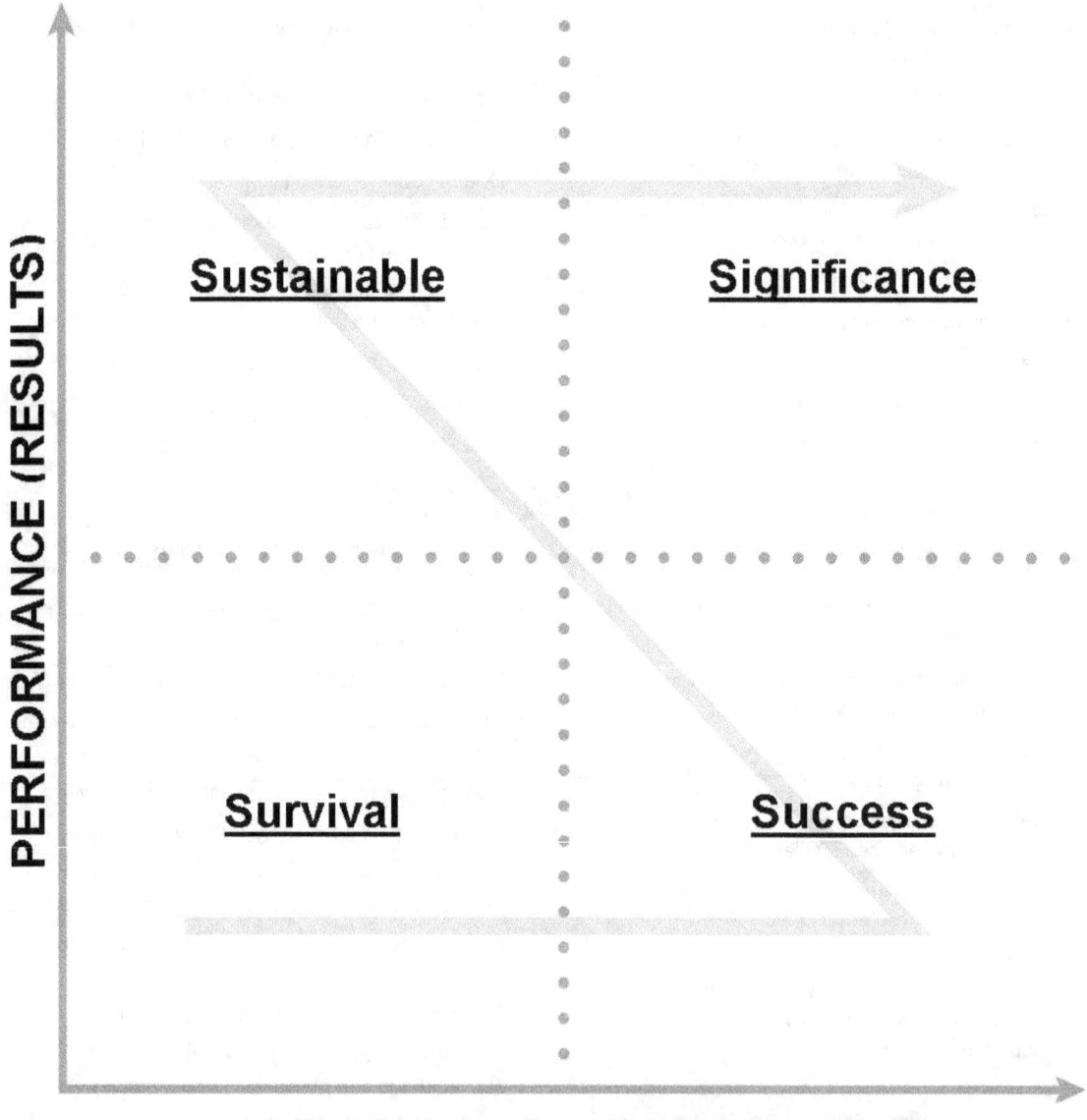

Build Sustainable Success
Reveal and Release Untapped Potential

"Whenever you see a successful business, someone once made a courageous decision."

~ Peter Drucker

PERFORMANCE (RESULTS)

Sustainable

- Client Profile 80% referrals based.
- Defined "A" level client profile.
- Annual client review process.
- Touch-point system to nurture client relationships.
- Effective CRM program.
- Clear vision, mission, goals.

Significance

- Working for meaning, not just money.
- Focused on making a difference.
- Clear profit formula (ROR).
- Partnership status with key clients (Lifetime Value).
- Well established business growth process.

WARRIOR SPIRIT

Survival

- Cold Calls.
- Direct mail.
- Observation prospecting.
- Networking.
- Basic record keeping system.

Success

- Written Business Plan.
- Referral Program.
- Develop Centers of Influence.
- Networking through associations.
- Repeatable personal selling system.
- Target Client Profile / Segmented Client List.

PROFESSIONAL DEVELOPMENT

Grow a Sustainable Business

Roadmap for building a successful, sustainable business.

LEADERSHIP FOCUS

Performance Culture

- Strategic thoughts and actions clearly defined in a written plan.
- Collaborative execution of strategy.
- Best practices and continuous improvement.
- Full utilization of available resources.
- Learning organization drives strategic innovation.

Leadership

- Shared vision across the organization.
- Positive, innovative corporate culture.
- Long-term sustainability.
- Customers view company as a strategic partner.
- Industry thought leader.
- Employee fulfillment.

Business Basics

- Disciplined thoughts and actions.
- Defined and documented practices and processes.
- Organizational structure established and functional roles clearly defined.

Customer & Employee Management

- Drive relationships with deep understanding of value proposition and competitive advantage.
- Innovative service and products create customer satisfaction.
- Model organizational values, strengthen individuals and culture.

PEOPLE FOCUS

Where are Your Customers or Prospects?

Where Do You Want Them to Be?

STRATEGICALLY IMPORTANT (vertical axis)

HARD TO REPLACE (horizontal axis)

Program

- Strong relationships and a plan.
- Innovative action plan with ongoing process improvements.
- Solid, functioning solutions.
- Reoccurring predictable revenue.

Partner and Value Creator

- Top of the mind—Part of planning with the client.
- Sustainable business with lifetime customer value.
- Client consults with you on major decisions.

Product

- Price focus is priority.
- RFP / bid situation.
- One of many vendors.

Preferred

- Great relationship.
- Always on the short list.
- Referral sources.

Your Work-Life Plan Accelerator

What is your work-life plan? Most often one will keep their work and personal life separate and compartmentalized. This is not realistic. People achieve higher levels of success and happiness when they learn to integrate their work and personal life. When *Both/And* thinking is used instead of *Either/Or* thinking, an individual will have new realizations and open themselves up to new possibilities and choices that will make lasting and enduring changes. Nature demonstrates *Both/And* thinking in how two rivers merge, which is referred to as confluence. For example, where the Mississippi and Ohio rivers merge the waters from each river do not mix together immediately. In fact you can view for a number of miles a distinct line of demarcation in the middle of the river. This is very evident when viewed by a satellite photo. It is three to five miles down river before the two rivers combine into the mighty Mississippi. This is what to expect from a Work-Life Plan. When one can stay focused on integrating their work and personal life, they will experience a much wider and expansive life in their work activities and personal life involvements. Use this framework to think thorough the primary aspects of both work and personal life. Write out your plans, strategies and dreams for both. As work and life progress through the years continue to review, refine and adjust. Share with others who are impacted by your dreams and goals.

	WORK PERFORMANCE ↑		**LIFE PLANNING** →
	Work Life Balance		Work-Life Purpose
	Business Vision		Community Involvement
	Business Plans & Strategies		Leadership
	Risk Management		Influence
	Manage Complexity		Financial Strategies
	Best Practices		Legacy
	Continuous Learning		Why You Do What You Do has Significance
	What you do has Excellence		
	Business Values		Values - Beliefs
	Best Behaviors		Convictions
	Basic Practices		Relationships: Family/Friends
	Personal Plans / Priorities		Win Friends & Influence People
	Professional Investment		Quality of Life
	Time Management		Health and Environment
	Daily Actions		Budget and Bucket List
	To Do and Stop Do Lists		Risk Avoidance
			Who You Are - Character

LIFE PLANNING

THE Ⓩ FACTOR

SALES ACCELERATOR

Got ZMap?

Send us your custom ZMap to:

ZMapIdeas@zfactorgroup.com

Sales Autobiography

Cindy G. Goldsberry

This closing section includes what I am calling my "Sales Autobiography". Every sales leader inevitably is asked to tell the story of what they have personally, actually sold—and the results they've produced. I get asked it all the time. So included below are highlights of my journey on the road of sales and to the destination of Value Creator…. it's really long—but you scan it for the parts that amuse and inspire you! You will notice my story is arranged by the *ZFactor Pathway to Success* to show my growth as a sales professional, going from Vendor to Value Creator,

Product Basics Phase

It was a really cold day, but I was prepared to go door to door and sell my wares. I was actually pretty excited. So I loaded the cart with my carefully laid out goods and headed out. The first door didn't answer. The second one shooed me away. But when I got to the third door—my neighbor, Miss Tina, bought $.50 cents worth of my hand knitted head warmers. I ended up making $2 during the hour or so I went door to door that afternoon. I was ecstatic. It was 1968. I was 9 years old. I didn't make $2 an hour until my first 'real' job in 1974 (minimum wage back then).

Okay… I'll fast forward a bit and include less detail in the novel of my life from here on. The simple question to be answered is, *"What have you sold and what have been your results?"* And so my story begins…

Cold Calling

My first sales job was as a headhunter placing geologists, geophysicists and land-men within the Permian Basin for Dorothy Roddy and Associates in Houston, Texas. Prior to that, all my life I had been told I should be a teacher, and I thought so too—and I was! I taught 6th grade in the NASA area of Houston for one year and loved it. Toward the end of that school year I walked into the teachers' lounge and saw a posting on the teachers' board showing what my pay potential would be after 20 years. It was less than double my salary at the time. Things have changed since then, obviously (If I were a teacher now I'd be making 4-6 times what I started at), but a switch went off in my head and I resigned within the next week for the upcoming school year. That's how I found the headhunting job the summer of 1982—I thought I was on my way to the top starting with glamorous offices in the Galleria on Westheimer. After all the oil industry was booming about then riding the increase in oil prices that rose in the 1981 timeframe!

My job, six hours a day, was cold calling to get interviews for our applicants with companies in the oil patch. I had two hours a day to 'sell' applicants on using our services and six hours a day to place them so I could get them work. I am a 20-something cold calling the rough and tough guys that ran the rigs and wells. The industry was just beginning to feel the massive drop in oil prices and number of working rigs. Each day, more and more unemployed professional geologists and geophysicists were showing up at our doors.

One of the worst (actually THE hardest, gut wrenching, painful, self esteem pain inflicting) things I have ever experienced was cold calling into the oil patch in an attempt to get an oil boss on the phone. Keep in mind that these guys were losing money and people—and watching business plummet before their eyes. My job was to ask if they had a need for a geologist or geophysicist and set up an interview.

One day I got a guy on the phone and—all I can say—is he ripped me a new one. WHO (swear word) was I to (swear word) STEAL his people, question his business...intervene...and (swear word) attempt to give him another (swear word) mouth to feed. I was crushed. I had, to that point in my life, never been verbally assaulted like that—complete with swear words, slurs on my character and challenges to my integrity. I was to too young to hang up on him because of my ode to the code of respect my elders.

I left my cubicle in a blubbering, slobbering mess, state of mind and flew to the bathroom. Other than Dorothy, I was the only other female in the firm. No one came to get me. No one came to comfort me or tell me it was okay. I rallied and got back on the phones. The following Monday I found out we were going straight commission and my salary would stop Friday.

That next weekend, I read the help wanted section of the paper and sent out seven *yellow* resumes. One of the jobs was for a recently acquired company by Motorola, called Four-Phase Systems. The job would begin with an eighteen month training program to become a Sales Systems Engineer selling minicomputers.

Getting Meetings and Selling Hardware

As it turned out, John Gordon*, the Sales Manager tasked to hire an applicant for this new and experimental management training program, had opened more than one hundred white resumes that day and had a stack of one hundred more to go through. Guess what happened when he opened my envelope and pulled out the yellow resume I'd prepared! I am pretty sure I was only called in because my resume was yellow. Remember – I had only had one year of teaching and just about three months of cold calling under my belt...

When I came in for the interview, I was escorted to a large room. Over fifty people sat at long tables lined against the walls filling out papers (mostly Asian men). Turned out this was an aptitude test of math, logic and communication skills (about ninety minutes) and was a prerequisite for the sales systems engineering position. There were two more interviews, a personality test and profiling after that. The process took about 3 weeks.

I got the job from a field of over one hundred qualified applicants. My starting salary was $10,000 more annually than my teaching salary. Over the next eighteen months I was trained to code computers – in ancient languages like Hexadecimal, COBOL, Fortran, Basic (LOL), and troubleshoot hardware, All

---

*   In 1990 Maj. John M. Gordon died when a C-5A plane crashed holding part-time soldiers who had volunteered to assist units deployed in the nation's Operation Desert Shield. They were transporting supplies for U.S. soldiers on alert in Saudi Arabia. He was from the 433rd Military Airlift Wing and served as the aircraft commander. John was a very special soul, and I will be forever thankful for having had him as a mentor in my life.

in ancient languages like Hexadecimal, COBOL, Fortran, Basic (LOL), troubleshoot hardware, and studied business principles and infrastructure of organizations – I received a mini business degree so to speak.

I was immersed in the practice of empirical observation and participated in an intensive sales training course that lasted three full-time weeks. This included sales methodology, business content and video recordings of sales presentations we made in role playing situations. Public critiques of our 'performances' were made one to three times a week in front of the entire classroom. Specifically, we were teamed up once or twice a day and traded off role playing a sales prospect scenario. The 'customer' would go into a meeting room with a desk and pull out the scenario of their situation. They had five minutes to decide the role they were going to take and what they thought they needed. The 'sales person' had twenty minutes to figure it out. I was #2 in a class of twenty-four folks (I missed #1 by a hair, mostly because I rebelled at one of the teaching methods I found to be incredibly ineffective. I was stupid, young and arrogant for doing that—I know. Sometimes to win, you just *have* to play by the rules—and I had not!). John was disappointed I had not gotten #1—but I think he was also rather amused that I'd taken such a hard stance (he got a call about it). I had graduated with a 4.0 from college—so getting a "B" so to speak was tough medicine for me.

Six months into the training (we alternated one month in Houston with the office team and one month living in Dallas going to school over the next eighteen months) I was assigned the oil and gas sector for the months I was in Houston. One Monday, I found a computer printout one inch thick with the names and numbers of the heads of technology in a set of assigned oil companies to target. Maybe some of you remember those fourteen inch wide, tractor-fed, green striped computer printouts? The cool thing was—I actually had a computer and a crude CRM system at my disposal and this is when I began to learn the importance of time management, contact management and the importance of creating a sales system for follow up.

I learned very, very quickly that NO one in an oil refinery or production facility wanted to hear what a blonde, twenty-three year old 'girl' had to say about mini-computers or business. Remember—it was still the really *good old boy* network back then and many of the IT shops were all legacy systems as well. Oh sure, they'd meet with me—no problem! But they'd just look at me and smile (you can imagine I was hit on quite a bit too since harassment and politically correct behaviors were but concepts at the time). For the industry sector, at that time, I had about as much of a chance being successful as of a snowball lasting a few minutes on the scorching August pavement in Houston.

I DID figure out that they would take a meeting and see me. I could get appointments! My record was sixteen, in person, meetings in one week. I averaged eight to ten meetings a week when in town. I made a deal with the resident thirty-five year old 'brain' in the office—and took Byron with me on calls... of course much to the surprise and chagrin of our prospect (at first). We were a heck of a team. I would open the door and he would close. I got an award for "Best at getting her foot in the door" and $150 to spend on new shoes. I don't know what our sales performance was specifically, but I know our office was on the map.

I had figured out the basics of time management, learning my products and making the calls to get appointments. And, more importantly, I had the horse sense to stop doing what didn't work and find the person 'who did' know what to do.

Preferred Status Phase

Demonstrating and Selling the Value of Technology

John left Motorola two years later and went to work for an Office Automation company called Syntrex and took me with him. My territory was all law offices South of McKinney in downtown Houston. I would literally load one of the first PC-type word processors on a cart (about forty pounds) and go office to office attempting to get receptionists to allow me to plug it in and show them how the wonders of Word Processing trumped a typewriter. I've been kicked out of many buildings and have lots of stories about how I'd start the day with my suit on and then change out my tie (remember the big hair and female bow ties of the 80's?, take off my jacket, put a bow in my hair...all so that the guards would miss me passing one more time (I'd memorize the marquee of a building and start on a floor and come down to find out where to go next).

One of my largest sales was a $100,000 local area network, connecting sixteen legal secretaries (that's what we called them back then) to a redundant server that hosted Word Processing on a dual DOS and CP/M system. I remember literally pulling a typewriter out of a sobbing secretary's hands who was resisting the evolution of technology. I had to get the final components of the network installed to get paid! The company didn't require it, but I began hosting informal training at my clients offices—much more focused on the 'cultural' needs of the women (again it was all women) who were migrating to such new tools. This led to referrals because Office Manager's knew of one another—especially among the major law firm players of that time. Clients began to recognize me as a value creator.

I convinced corporate to send me to the Hannover Fair in Europe to work our booth at the technology pavilion (I was fluent in German back then)—and as you can imagine, it didn't hurt that I was tall, young and blonde. You have to work with what you have! I am most proud however, that the company selected me to be Master of Ceremonies and primary presenter at a conference we put on to review best practices in office automation. We did a blitz of over one thousand companies and had over two hundred folks in attendance.

Selling the Company Value Prop and Professional Services

Through a series of referrals and my friend Sharon at Syntrex (I wasn't looking for a job) I was hired by Arthur Young as a consultant in their new Information Technology Group in Houston. They had received a contract to support eight Entre' Computer Centers, which was a new concept in training corporation personnel. I traveled around Houston and taught courses all day to professionals for Lotus, DisplayWrite...and yes...DOS. Isn't it fascinating how everything we do layers upon itself? My degree and experience in teaching coupled with the training and exposure I had in office automation and technology is what landed that opportunity for me.

I spent two years as a billed consultant on office automation projects for corporations, and my role changed many times over the next five and a half years. My final position was at a Manager level. As far as a 'sales' focus to be pertinent for these purposes—I began 'selling' myself into internal roles as a change agent for internal training, development and recruiting for the organization. Literally I would propose a new position, pitch it and either get that job or not. I experienced (and survived) the fascinating merger between Arthur Young and Ernst and Whinney.

One of the first major changes was responsibility for recruiting data processing professionals to be consultants for the Southeast region of E&Y—so I was selling recruits on E&Y. Over eighteen months, we grew from fifteen to over eighty professionals in Houston and more than six hundred in the entire region. I managed all advertising and marketing to obtain recruits, scanned over two thousand resumes (yes on paper), coordinated nearly two hundred interviewees (each had a minimum of four interviews and we had no email, text or IM at the time); and facilitated sixty-seven offers with fifty-six accepting.

In 1988 with the help of my manager in Dallas, we started the *High Tech Cooperative* in Houston, by engaging the recruiting managers of thirty plus Fortune 100 companies to join a networking group so we could share resumes. Many of the oil companies and such just needed "geeks" that could code. E&Y needed folks we could dress up and bill out at $85 an hour. Remember—we didn't have LinkedIn, Facebook, Google+ or even email back then! This all happened by phone, mail and fax.

Together, this group held the very first *High Tech Career Fair* in Houston with three thousand attendees. I remember so well getting in trouble because I was interviewed on TV wearing a fuchsia suit. It *should* have been navy blue suit to fit the corporate dress code. I have always thought a little differently.

Additional projects included managing a project to build the first *time and billing system* that integrated consultants in sixteen cities and provided weekly reporting on billed and projected hours. This resulted in a report that twenty partners reviewed on Mondays to track and report utilization of consultants in the region (essentially sales results and projections). I managed a $350,000 training budget and traveled the nation training data programmers on how to be consultants. My job was to introduce the attributes of interpersonal skills, questioning strategies and basic sales techniques to these folk to use in their consulting (a big part of moving up the ladder). In 1989 I received the #1 training instructor of the year from a field of over fifty instructors—many of the instructors were Partners. During this time I married my high school sweetheart in 1983 and divorced him in 1986. I met Alan in 1986 and we were married on Halloween 1987.

I think of this time as my 'INtrapreneur' period. Look up Intrapreneurship on Wikipedia. I'll make it easy for you:1992,*The American Heritage Dictionary* defines the popular use of a new word, intrapreneur, to mean "A person within a large corporation who takes direct responsibility for turning an idea into a profitable finished product through assertive risk-taking and innovation." Intrapreneurship is now known as the practice of a corporate management style that integrates risk-taking and innovation approaches, as well as the reward and motivational techniques that are more traditionally thought of as being the province of entrepreneurship."

Selling Consumer Products

I got pregnant in 1990 and E&Y had a reorganization, so I took a package to move on. I used my severance to start *One Slim Cookie*, a nutritional cookie company, with a partner. It was one of the first meal replacement concepts for a high protein, low fat product. We raised money, used MRE (meals ready to eat) packaging for the cookies, as a way to extend shelf life and established a multi-level sales organization. Our San Antonio bakery had made food for Desert Storm and was downsizing as the war was unwinding. About one year into the enterprise the cookie crumbled. It was here I learned the hard way on how stupid investments in marketing do not create sales! One Slim Cookie was founded in Houston, TX—and not to be confused with any other existing company with the same name.

The company we were leasing space from, *Biogime Skin Care of Entourage International* (now RevitaCell) wanted to add vitamins and nutritional supplements to their product line. So, using my experience with the nutritional cookie, I worked with laboratories and manufacturing, marketing and branding strategists to develop the NutriSense line of products complete with an ester C, antioxidants (this was so new back then), and a Balanced B formula. I loved, loved, loved doing the research and pouring myself into authentic nutritional formulas. I loved working on the mark-up and profit scenarios, challenged by producing margin on product sold that might have six levels of payout in the commission structure. We had to create all the marketing and promotion to sell the sales channel on selling the products. We launched to two thousand independent multi-level, skin care professionals. Our first month we did $10,000 in sales, which was pennies in the scheme of things, but was a huge shot in the arm for overall revitalization of the sales force with new products and a new reason to talk to customers.

I then was offered the position of National Marketing Director for the Biogime sales organization and am thankful for the mentoring from one of the original leaders at Biogime, Carla. I redesigned the commission plan, recreated and updated training and video advertorials used for recruiting and selling and traveled the nation doing Rah-Rah events—trained and sold with sales professionals. The toughest part of the job was the huge cultural diversity of the straight commission sales channel. There was a wide array of people and levels of knowledge, expertise, professionalism, commitment, and discipline for sales. I was only thirty-one years old, and many of the 'old guard' didn't necessarily like a young pup out in front. We exceeded our numbers and I earned the first bonus (not a commission) of my career.

The layering of my career continued to prepare me for what's next—from teacher to sales, learning to leverage technology, big and small company experience and leading a large independent sales organization. I was learning how to put it all together, yet there was still more to learn to prepare me for who I am today. Looking back, it is easy to see how each stage of my journey developed and prepared me for what's next.

Program Mastery Phase

Selling Retail and Managing Advertising

Alan and I ended up buying a *Biogime Skin Care* franchise for the Southeast Region and moved to Atlanta, GA, in 1994, with a two and a half year and five month old sons. Our skin care center was in an A-grade retail space in the heart of Buckhead. We used infomercial advertising (can you say

Sham-WOW for skin care?) to sell as much as $50,000 a month of skin care out of about 1,200 sq. ft. space. We also did direct mail, POS offers, campaigns, extreme-networking and managed outbound calling (employees had to make seventy-five outbound calls a day). Surprising as it may seem, I am not cut out to sit in a retail store all day and wait for the door to chime.

We were master networkers and held multiple cross-business promotions in the Buckhead business district (our dry cleaner stapled skin care offers to dry cleaning bags, for example). Walk-ins received facials and we held events and parties in the space. I started the Women's Business Exchange (WBE) networking group and have several life-long relationships as a result—Linda, Catherine, Julie, Bonnie. Amazing local folks like *Dr. Bruce!* (Bruce Salzinger the chiropractor) were part of our beloved business village.

Through networking with the women in the community, I was invited to be one of four women who hosted a unique set of radio shows on WQXI 790am. This was the height of all the "hate talk radio" and we were tired of it. It was time for something positive and uplifting. We did block-programming, meaning we had to pay for the time ($150 per show). My initial motivation was I wanted to be able to say when I am eighty, "I did a live radio talk show." Literally—that is why I did it.

The show was called *"The Winning Attitude"* and initially used the show to promote the Skin Care business. Alan joined me after about four months and we created an offering to 'break even' on our cost. We expanded to offer other integrated advertising programs for businesses with whom we were net-working. We sold advertising and full media packages and gave local businesses the chance to be "on the radio". Interviewees on our show included local business owners and leaders and folks like Seth Godin, Jeffrey Gitomer, Mark Victor Hansen, Laurie Beth Jones, Dr. Ivan Misner and many others. We began to focus on thought leaders around a thing called the Internet. We had one of the first radio show websites and provided links to all our guests' websites, if they had one. If they didn't have a website, after being on our show, they did. One of the most successful give-aways was a 3.5" diskette that helped people set up a personal email.

Selling marketing, advertising and promotion services and events

At the height of the networking, we pulled it all together in a program called *Influence Atlanta*. Influence Atlanta had a board of business and media owners who collaborated to offer packages to include web, radio, community paper and a booth at a quarterly event for businesses networking. I and Julie who worked for me sold the packages with the Skin Care center as the home base. We also had some amazingly supportive men and women who helped the program immensely in being successful. It was perfect for local businesses. In 1995 the *Winning Attitude* website made USA today top three sites nationwide. In 1996 we held one of the first Internet events in Atlanta, themed, *"WWW – Wonder What's Working?"* By now Alan and I had founded Sales Performance Technologies—which was the parent company for all these activities.

As fate would have it, the franchisor of our skin care centers (Entourage – a public company) had a proxy battle and huge challenges with management. The support for the franchise and infusion of marketing for the infomercial business model became non-existent and we had to close first—and then a second location…essentially before we had expanded much in the region. Overnight, infomercials were in demand and rates went from $1,000 per show to $4,000 per show. I learned when things change, they can change, fast. We lost hundreds of thousands of dollars in the investment. I began to fail in my ability to manage the various businesses—skin care, radio show, Influence Atlanta, and deliver on the promises I had made. In addition—and not an excuse, but our boys were now six and three years old. All in all—I failed at everything at that time in my life—and especially in taking care of my husband, my children and the amazing friends and business associates who were there for us. To the folks that were there and supported us personally and professionally, I am forever grateful.

Financially, we lost so much during that time. Personally we lost face…and some emotional skin, but we had a lot of great skincare product! Those were tough times financially, personally and spiritually. But Alan and I made it through—Thank you God.

Selling tradeshows, events, print, and early web applications

One of the primary sponsors of *Influence Atlanta* was *Jaye Communications* (now www.techlinks.net). One day Mike called to tell me he had committed to do a high tech career expo in and for his Technology Magazine. At eleven weeks away, not a single booth had been sold, nor sponsor obtained, nor did he have a plan to drive traffic to the event other than the magazine and web presence.

In eleven weeks, April (a Techlinks sales rep) and I sold thirty-eight booths at $2,500 each (it was really April doing the closing, as I did the marketing and advertising to 'tee' prospects up for contracts). I have extremely fond memories of hearing and yelling 'incoming' when one or the other of us got a company hooked. We even posted caricatures and cartoons of us wearing helmets and yelling 'incoming' from the 'pit' of battle around the office. You have to know that in working with Mike—that's just the way you had to roll! He has quite the military career. His bio does not say how many times he was shot down *behind* enemy lines and survived…I think it was thirteen.

We took some internet code that had been developed by the guys in the back office and pulled together a data bank to host a virtual job fair online at the same times as the expo—one of the first of its kind. We called the site USjobnetwork.com and attracted about four hundred folks online and another four hundred to the event in person (I do not know for sure if the original usjobnetwork we had is the legacy of the current one or not). The event, though small in traffic, was highly successful.

After that, I managed the initiative to officially launch USjobnetwork.com to recruiting managers on a subscription basis. Alan became involved in the business as well and we had about $10,000 a month in reoccurring monthly subscriptions by the second month—with one employee who managed it all. Next, I worked with the team to help launch Techlinks magazine and we built one of the early digital web based magazine companion sites. We sold advertising packages integrating the print and web based products. Figuring out revenue down to the quarter page, walking the hallways to see the layout of the magazine on the walls (because the software couldn't do that back then) and determining how many signatures we could go to print with and make a profit—was all in all, an amazing experience. Pulling it all together and pricing the integrated print and web-based advertising packages to prospects who had NEVER purchased such was more than interesting and challenging. Calculating profit was not easy with only an Excel spreadsheet back then—but we did it!

At this stage of my career, it may appear that I could be in my late forties to early fifties, yet I was thirty-eight. Not quite a twenty year career, yet it is clear how my career journey is the ZFactor pathway. Up to this point, I had mastered the quadrants of Product Basics, Preferred Status and Program Mastery. It is amazing to look back over these years and see the small, but defining moments that led to literally quantum leaps in my career...such as noticing the Teachers' wage chart, deciding to send out *yellow* resumes, and there being any number of what appeared to be chance meetings or being blessed by numerous mentors. Again, all this came together to prepare me for the journey to Value Creator.

Value Creator

Selling technology and enterprise solutions

Through networking, I ended up accepting a position in 1997 with *HomeCom Communications*, one of the industry's first web development companies. I was hired to run marketing and communications in preparation for the company's IPO. I know that sounds like a huge leap—what...you mean from 6th grade teacher to Director of MarCom for an Internet company IPO? When you treat people well, you genuinely care about them and authentically create value for them—it is easy to see the Butterfly Effect of all we do layers upon itself to create new opportunities!

As the IPO approached, my job was to pull together branding, marketing and communications into one unified corporate structure for meeting the needs of growing clients and investors. Over a five month period of time our team built the machine for vetting and retaining professional Public Relations, Investor Relations and a Creative Design firm. We engaged with the Gartner Group and put an extensive industry research and positioning plan in motion. We completely transformed the brand and image of the company (which had been positioned for internet hosting accounts) and replaced all associated guidelines and print and electronic collateral. We designed and launched a new website and layered interactivity in the site for meeting web audiences with specific content meant for their needs. We laid the foundation for recruiting and hiring a new sales force to sell Internet technology products (Personal Banking, coding, security, etc.); designed and launched a robust series of marketing campaigns to successfully result in significant leads within the Fortune 100 space.

I managed a $1MM marketing budget and a matrix of direct reports, interdepartmental staff, a variety of service providers and coordinated interviews and investor road shows and events. My cold calling experiences gave me a leg up on the tough skin required to field investor calls to be sure! These were fast and wild times to be sure. One of my favorite memories was managing the 'feedback' from having run advertising on the Howard Stern radio show as part of one blitz promotion. I was the only woman on a brilliant fourteen person management team reporting to the CEO, Harvey.

My team and key folks in creative were rock stars. I will be forever beholden to Mitchell (now with his own company (www.holmesinnovations.com) and others who spun at a "great team" pace.

Selling professional services, systems and solutions

I was at HomeCom about six months and ended up handing the reigns over for several reasons. The first was that while I was qualified to build out the machine—ultimately my experience was not enough for running and growing MarCom for a public company. Also—I just couldn't keep up the pace with two small children and the stress took its toll on me. I did maintain a relationship and managed many other projects over the next year or so on contract under the umbrella of Sales Performance Technologies—the company Alan and I had started a few years earlier.

Over the next six years. I sold consulting services as a 'free lance' VP of sales and marketing for small business. This was a great time. I worked with companies and divisions of larger corporations who needed help but didn't have the sales and marketing expertise on staff. I've started with just a business plan and have worked in creating marketing campaigns for lead generation, developing sales strategies, pitches, presentations, training and built tracking and reporting programs. Work included doing presentations for clients to their customers, executive coaching, writing copy, revamping websites, selling a $50,000 annually licensed extranet, etc. Over those years I worked with over thirty other companies to understand their product or service, their culture, their ideal customer and helped design the *Go-To-Market* marketing materials and sales tools required to engage new clients through the creation of value. Alan and I desperately wanted to get back to Texas, and in 1998 we were able to do so. Two primary clients, one based in New York and the other in Michigan, were fine with wherever I chose to live! It was the dawning of the virtual, collaborative organization.

Serving a Channel of Sales Professionals

Once again, through networking, is how I connected with HotLink in 2000—and Jason Black who wrote the Foreword of this book. HotLink was Jason's first company and as a true visionary, Jason needed help getting marketing deliverables over the goal line (and in he's own words, "I am never short of ideas!"). He literally said that to me in our first meeting. HotLink had proprietary, in-house, web-based software that automated and controlled ordering of promotional products. Essentially this was one of the first "Online Company Stores" with a bit more to it. They had a handful of clients and thus proof of concept that clients wanted and needed the technology.

I worked on and off as a contractor with HotLink over the next three years. I created marketing materials, worked with the sales team and eventually collaborated with Jason to bring the "MarketPlace" platform to market and expand it beyond just a few accounts to be a full web-based product offering for clients. In 2003 we landed a seven figure RFP with a major healthcare company in Texas, and I closed up my consulting and went full-time with HotLink. We were successful in securing many large contracts and had the opportunity to work with such brands as Dell, Bechtel, Travelocity, Administaff (now Insperity) and E&J Gallo. We sold licensing fees for the technology and built an internal department to manage $200,000 annually in reoccurring revenue for the platform. During this time the early foundation of the *ZFactor* methodology was introduced to the sales team and was used in my personal strategy for growing what we began to call 'Enterprise Sales'.

Jason left in 2005 to start Boundless Network and was successful in securing a 'left brain' (Henrik Johansson) and professional capital to take the vision he has for transforming the promotional products industry to the next level. I joined the company as VP of Sales and Marketing in March of 2006, after declining a position as VP Marketing for another technology company in Austin. At the time, Boundless had done $800K in sales in 2005 and had eleven sales professionals. The entire corporate staff could fit in a 10x10 conference room. Our initial management meetings were Mondays at a coffee shop on Congress Avenue. I have never regretted my decision to be with Boundless!

From Success to Significance

Over the last six years I have held several roles leading up to my current role now as VP Strategic Sales and Services. In the early years we were *all* involved in everything—it was all hands on deck for marketing, sales, recruiting, on boarding, event management and sales training and systems. We could have never done it all without Courtney, Nancy, Mark and Liz...and many others.

In 2008 it became clear there was a new level of strategic value we could bring to clients. Because of our investors and especially our team, we had a real opportunity to evolve the perception of our industry as 'koozie salesmen' to sales professionals who help companies manage and control their branding and promotional spending. We had a technology platform and patents coming that were powerful differentiators. So, we embarked on what we called "Enterprise Account Sales (EAS)" which is our strategic approach to working with clients. EAS has now evolved to being called Strategic Accounts (because you don't have to start at the enterprise level necessarily to be strategic).

As a result of this focus, we have had several generations (classes) of sales professionals progressing through coaching and training—much of it based on the ZFactor methodology. Many are not keenly aware of that, but the vocabulary is interwoven into the fabric of our conversations. My greatest joy and sense of accomplishment is in seeing the amazing success of our people. We have been so blessed by the talent that has come on board with Boundless over the years. They are the cream-of-the-crop of the industry.

Starting with $800K in sales in 2005, the company did $43MM in 2011. Strategic Accounts (where we are locked in as Value Creators) were less than $1MM in sales in 2008 and now comprise 32% of Boundless revenues—meaning predictability of revenue and loyalty for both our team and clients. In early 2009 I became a Survivor of breast cancer and the management team and board of directors graciously allowed me to revise my responsibilities to meet the new demands of a more balanced lifestyle. My role over the last three years has been pretty much all about driving success and value for our sales professionals and clients. It's a dream come true.

However, that is not to say it's been a slow pace these last few years! The initial health challenges forced me to *Re-Think* my way of conducting business. From a business perspective, the health challenges became the opportunity for me to step back from the day-to-day and think differently about how I needed to act differently. As I did this, much of my prior experience became ever-more relevant.

Believe me. I know the process of *Rebooting your Mindset* is definitely an accelerator to performance. Thinking and acting differently is a daily practice for me because sales growth is accelerating, as this book goes to print. Current close ratio is approaching 86% of major enterprise RFPs. Goals are to double sales from $12MM to $25MM in the next couple of years. As my health returned, it may appear I simply learned to be smart about leveraging technology and utilizing various online tools. It's an interesting thing about tools. Anyone can learn to use a tool, but only a few truly master the full capabilities of the tool and utilize the tools in such a way that creates value and new possibilities for others.

During this time I've learned what it means to be the *'wind beneath' a sales professional's wings*. They laugh every time I say it. They may just be being nice, but it is an amazing blessing to see the foundations of my passion for teaching manifest in such rich relationships of significance. I hope those same wings spread far and wide for you and that the Butterfly Effect takes on a new dimension for all you sell, all you do and every life you touch.

About the Authors

Cindy G. Goldsberry, Author

Cindy G. Goldsberry has thirty years of Sales, Marketing and Training experience, specifically in developing and implementing sales-generating marketing and business strategies for entrepreneurial companies and startups. Her experience extends to many industries and departments within an organization.

As a manager with Ernst & Young in the late 1980s, her 6-year tenure took her through managing office automation projects to primary responsibility for the systems to track people and knowledge assets in the Information Technology Group of Ernst & Young's Southeast region. Her career then took her to other technology companies and startups to include being VP of MarCom for one of the first Internet IPOs in the late 1990's. She either worked within or served as an advisor/consultant/coach to over 30 startups and small companies, including two of her own businesses.

Most recently, Cindy has been VP of Strategic Sales at Boundless Network, an Austin Ventures portfolio company. She joined the founders in 2006; the sales organization has grown from 11 sales professionals to over 150, and sales have grown from $800K in 2005 to $43MM in 2011.

She celebrates being a survivor of breast cancer, is a advisor/mentor to the Young Women's Forum (a Gen Y professional women's group), is a student of cross-generational dynamics and diversity and an advocate for work-life balance for women in the workplace. She has been married to the love of her life since 1987, and has two fabulous sons in college. They are the reason she colors her hair.

Alan W. Goldsberry, Advisor and ZFactor Creator

Alan's sales and business building career spans nearly forty years. He acquired his basic sales skills by selling door-to-door with Southwestern Company and started his first business in 1977, from a business plan he wrote while attending a small business management class at the University of Texas.

Alan firmly believes sales mastery is essential for building any business. As Alan's sales skills and business practices developed and matured, he built several companies from small private companies to taking a company public. He knows fast-growth as a co-founder of Allied Waste Industries. In the first eighteen months from startup, the company went from one garbage truck and three employees to thirty garbage trucks and one hundred and ten employees. Business activity went from operating a few hours a week to running 24x7. Alan remained with the company for eleven years, as it grew through multiple acquisitions and mergers. Soon after Alan resigned from the board of directors to pursue another startup, Allied acquired BFI Industries. Allied later merged into Republic Services, Inc. in 2008. Alan has held positions of director, chairman, executive and advisor for multiple startups and has coached or mentored executives and business owners, in various industries.

During the last ten years, he has lead the development of the ZFactor sales and coaching methodology from a proprietary *XY* framework entitled Leader*XY* Framework. Alan is a graduate of the University of Texas and lives in Austin, Texas with his wonderful wife Cindy. Their marriage of almost twenty-five years is blessed by their amazing sons. TK and Alec are in college.